# The Horse Behaviour Handbook

## Abigail Hogg

David & Charles

*In memory of Rico, who was shot for being afraid.*

A DAVID & CHARLES BOOK

First published in the UK in 2003

Copyright © Abigail Hogg 2003

Distributed in North America
by F&W Publications, Inc.
4700 East Galbraith Road
Cincinnati, OH 45236
1-800-289-0963

A catalogue record for this book is available from the British
Library.

ISBN 0 7153 1467 X

Printed in the UK by Bulter & Tanner Limited
for David & Charles
Brunel House    Newton Abbot    Devon

Commissioning Editor: **Jane Trollope**
Project Editor: **Sarah Widdicombe**
Desk Editor: **Shona Wallis**
Art Editor: **Sue Cleave**
Production Controller: **Ros Napper**

Visit our website at www.davidandcharles.co.uk

David & Charles books are available from all good bookshops;
alternatively you can contact our Orderline on (0)1626 334555
or write to us at FREEPOST EX2110, David & Charles Direct,
Newton Abbot, TQ12 4ZZ (no stamp required UK mainland).

# Contents

# Introduction: Simple Creatures

*'But if we would see him in the enjoyment of his native freedom, (unsubdued by the restraint man has imposed upon him) we must look for him in the wild and extensive plains... where he ranges without controul [sic], in a state of entire independency.'*

A General History of Quadrupeds *(1790), Thomas Bewick*

There is no animal of which we ask so much as the horse. Many of our requests run counter to the horse's natural behaviour, yet despite this, if treated well he will strive to understand and co-operate. However, everyone who deals with these animals will at some time reach the point of asking 'Why?' in response to a horse's actions. This book aims to address this question.

In fact, horses are very simple creatures if you look at them in *their* world. They are herbivores, whose main preoccupations are to eat as much as possible and to avoid being eaten themselves. However, they are big animals. When they misunderstand and are misunderstood they react emotionally; then, their size makes them dangerous and we become afraid of them. So we restrain and control them.

From childhood, much of what I was told about horses did not make sense to me. Why lead them from the left? Why should their manes be on the right side of the neck? Why keep them shut in stables for long periods of time? Why put pieces of metal in their mouths to control them? These were rules, almost laws, which had to be accepted without explanation.

There was only one voice I came across that was saying anything different. As a teenager, I read *The Horse's Mind* by Lucy Rees. This book dismissed the irrational rules. It explained about the horse as an animal in its own right, starting from the obvious

place – the horse in the wild. This approach helped me to understand why my horses behaved as they did, and I successfully applied Lucy's ideas about handling and treating horses more humanely to my own ponies. Sixteen years later, I had the opportunity to spend a summer as Lucy's student as she toured around Spain, running courses and workshops, and working with horses that had problems.

The horses I met and worked with helped answer many of my questions, and made me ask many more. Some were animals whose owners could get nowhere with them – horses that would not or could not be controlled using the faulty ideas about equine psychology being applied to them. When horses get to this stage, humans throw up the hands and the only solution becomes a bullet. However, by looking at the horses as *horses*, alternatives can be found.

This book is, in part, an exploration of the real nature of horses. The behaviour of wild horses has been documented in detail in Joel Berger's comprehensive study *The Horses of the Great Basin*, and this has informed many of the ideas I have put forward in this book. I have also studied scientific papers, particularly when researching the reasons for abnormal behaviours. And I am, of course, eternally grateful to Lucy Rees for sharing her knowledge with me.

I hope this book will be of use to everyone who has contact with horses, and anyone who wants to become more involved with them. My aim is to help other people escape from the domination of so-called experts and start looking for their own answers to questions, so that our relationships with horses can be improved. My hope is that this book will be a step in the right direction.

# 1 The Foundations of Horse Behaviour

*'Give me your definition of a horse.'* Mr Gradgrind in Hard Times, *Charles Dickens*

There are as many answers to Mr Gradgrind's question as there are people involved with horses. The reply to the schoolmaster comes back: 'Quadruped. Gramnivorous. Forty teeth, namely twenty-four grinders, four eye-teeth, and twelve incisive.' Which, like many definitions we may hear, does not help us at all in trying to understand why our horses behave as they do.

The horse's natural behaviour consists of eating, drinking, sheltering, socializing, breeding, resting and avoiding danger. The psychology of the horse has evolved to enable the animal to live in a certain way, yet most of our horse-keeping practices and activities are unnatural. We control every part of their lives, from the time at which they do things, to whom they can interact with and how they move. Everything we do with horses involves some modification of their behaviour, yet the need to act naturally remains in all horses.

Even in domestic situations, where nutritional needs are usually met, horses need to exhibit a range of natural behaviours in order to be psychologically balanced. These can be reduced to three main requirements: spending most of their time feeding, being with other horses, and moving.

Whatever we do to horses, whether we call them champion show ponies, premium sires or best friends, we cannot change their basic nature. However much we believe that they can adapt to living in captivity, they will always need to spend time engaging in the activities they are 'hard wired' to carry out. In many ways, the three needs mentioned above are indivisible; they all arise from the horse's existence in his natural environment. The loss of these three foundations leads to problems, both physical and psychological.

# Feeding

Given the choice, horses spend about 16 hours of their time every day looking for food and eating it. If food is hard to come by, they will spend more time. Rarely will they spend less. This allocation of time changes little whatever the system under which horses live. A horse's mental health depends on the amount of time he can spend chewing. This may sound odd, but horses do not act like humans or predators with regard to food. A horse doesn't wait until he is hungry to look for food: he eats at every opportunity. A horse's passion is to find food and eat it. The search for food is an active process involving moving from place

to place, testing different plants, digging for roots or grass under snow, and flicking aside dead leaves or unpalatable plants. In the wild, this is a full-time job and one for which the horse is designed.

Horses have evolved to eat food of low nutritional value. They are better survivors than other large herbivores, such as cattle. In the growing season, the horse's job is to eat as much as possible in order to get fat; in winter, this fat is what will keep him alive. So, winter or summer, the premium on time is to forage. Grass, herbs, moss, fruit, bark and mud – the

horse's diet is varied to ensure an intake of different nutrients, and a clever horse is one that maximizes successful eating time. The mares that take in the highest levels of nutrition are the most successful in producing foals, thereby ensuring their contribution to the survival of the species.

By keeping horses in stables, we limit the time they spend eating and searching for food, and their ability to choose a variety of foods. For an animal whose main occupation is eating, restricting his access to food is quite serious. In behavioural terms, the most obvious consequence of restricting feeding behaviour is the development of mouth-focused abnormal behaviours in horses. Crib-biting, wood-chewing and tongue-lolling are all ways that horses find to occupy their mouths.

■ **Mare and foal in perfect horse country**
This foal is growing up in a group of horses, has other foals to play with, and spends his time cantering up and down scree slopes that act as a training ground. The moorland pasture is ideal horse food and the mare is in good condition.

## Unnatural Systems

In domestic situations, we have systems that run counter to the horse's natural way of feeding.

○ We often reduce the eating time to a quarter or less of the time horses would naturally spend foraging.

○ We feed highly concentrated food, so we have to feed less of it.

○ We restrict the variety of food on offer; forage is always the same, normally hay or haylage.

○ Horses kept at grass are usually on improved pasture that is designed for agricultural animals producing meat or milk. The grass is too high in nutrients for horses, so we have to restrict their intake.

# Companionship

Horses never choose to live alone. The survival advantage of living together is that there is safety in numbers, but horses are also motivated emotionally by a strong desire for company. Free-living horses strive to live together: bachelor stallions make friends with other bachelors, mares live in groups with their young of various ages.

Horses interact constantly with each other. They are always in full visual contact with another horse and have regular physical contact. They touch and play, they follow each other. They form strong friendships, particularly with siblings, and these one-to-one relationships may last a lifetime. Friends will stay physically close to each other, engaging in mutual grooming and grazing side by side. If separated, they become distressed.

A group of horses has an internal coherence. The members synchronize perfectly. When one turns, so do the rest, like a flock of birds. They co-ordinate one-to-one (for example, by constantly adjusting their personal distances) and to benefit the group (for example, by one member standing to keep watch while the rest lie down). This cohesion of a group of horses can be seen when they detect danger: it can be difficult to tell which horse moves first because the whole group runs, and stops, as one.

A foal is born into a society from which he learns the information he needs in order to survive. The band of horses knows where to find food, water and shelter, and what is dangerous and what is not, so the foal's education begins from day one. Most foals are born with kicking and biting as their natural defence against unwanted attention that may hurt them; over time, older horses teach younger ones about social behaviour. Respect for body space is a primary lesson and one that has consequences for

humans. How often are we crowded or barged by horses that simply do not understand the limits of our personal distance? How often do we invade their body space without noticing their reaction?

In the herd young horses learn how to approach other horses, and also how to engage in courtship: woe betide any strutting colt who thinks he can march up to a mature mare and jump on her. These are lessons that remain with them for ever. So, if we can socialize our horses as clearly as other horses do, tell them what we want and do not want from them without being confusing, and build on each lesson, we are well on the way to a relationship with our horses that is mutually satisfying.

Wild horses experience a whole area of life that is completely denied to most domestic horses, even those used for breeding, and that is a sex life. Growing up in a herd gives horses the chance to learn about the opposite sex. Courtship and mating are observed from an early age; young stallions are usually of little interest to mature mares, young fillies of little interest to mature stallions. It is often the mares who initiate contact and dictate when sex will take place, and they will actually seek out the stallion.

In contrast, most domestic horses have no sex life at all. When geldings and mares are kept separately there is no opportunity for flirting, and

geldings that mount mares are frowned upon. The common method of breeding allows no courtship. The mare is often hobbled and twitched, and sometimes blindfolded; she is not given the opportunity to turn and look at the stallion, let alone have any contact. If a mare is lucky, she will be spared this trauma and inseminated artificially instead. The luckiest mares of all are those who nip over the wall into the field with the pony next door and get on with the process away from human interference.

Many stallions are kept virtually as machines to produce semen, living permanently in their loose-boxes and brought out only when needed to cover mares. Some stallions mate mostly with a dummy mare or false vagina, to allow collection of semen for artificial insemination. Stallions kept in these ways have no social life at all.

■ **Social interaction**
This filly had just met two bachelor colts and returned to her parents for reassurance. Horses are highly social animals with complex relationships. They need to see, touch and interact with other horses.

# Space to Move

Having the space to move is central to a horse's sense of security. In order to survive he must escape danger, and to escape he needs to run. A horse that is tied or enclosed cannot run – his main defence has been neutralized and so he feels vulnerable. Horses also need space to move away from each other. Keeping too many horses in one place leads to higher levels of aggression than are seen in free-ranging horses.

When a free-living horse eats, he also moves.

❍ A domestic horse travels constantly when grazing, but covers nowhere near the distance of a

free-living horse, which may need to travel many miles each day for water and whose food is spread out over a large area.

○ Moving to feed keeps a horse supple, as he often has to stretch his body in order to reach food and to graze up and down slopes.

○ The horse has evolved to eat with his head down, so the top and bottom jaw are aligned in this position, thereby allowing the teeth to wear down evenly. (In addition, unlike concentrated feeds, grasses contain particles of silica that aid the wearing process.)

○ When grazing, the horse's weight is constantly being transferred from leg to leg, maintaining the circulation of the blood and aiding the healing of any injuries.

Horses, both young and old, need to play. For youngsters, playing prepares them for adult life. It improves co-ordination, increases stamina and builds muscle. Play also allows horses to practise running away and fighting, and to try out sexual behaviour.

In the domestic situation, not only do we overfeed horses but we also restrict their movement by shutting them in stables. They often have no outlet for their high energy levels and no space to run, to buck and to roll. It is no wonder that we end up with horses suffering from the equine equivalent of hyperactivity disorders. An hour's exercise barely gets a horse warmed up, let alone tires him. Restricted exercise, such as lunging with side reins, does not allow the animal to frolic. Unnatural exercises, such as controlled dressage movements, are mentally tiring and increase the need for a horse to have freedom and time to himself away from human control.

Being free to move also has physiological consequences that affect both mental and physical health. Importantly, a horse at liberty spends most of his time with his head below his withers, which is the position horses are designed to be in.

Taking account of the natural needs of horses to feed, socialize and move around not only improves their lives but also enhances our relationship with them, increasing the satisfaction we gain from working with them.

**■ Born to move**
These young horses take delight in running together. Movement is how horses express themselves and communicate.

# A Domestic Foal – Early Socialization

Let's briefly consider how the life of a typical domestic youngster differs from that described on page 10.

A foal is born straight into human expectations: the foal's human-prescribed 'purpose' in life, whether as a show pony, racehorse or trotter, will be what governs his upbringing, rather than the simple fact that he is a horse. A domestic foal is often born into a social group that consists only of his mother or possibly a few other mares and foals as well. They are kept separate from other horses in case the foals get harmed. The foal has no opportunity to interact with his father or observe sexual behaviour.

If a foal is lucky, there will be other foals to play with; if not, he spends time trying to play with his mother, who tolerates his invasion of her body space in a way that no other horse would, because he is her baby. So, the foal does not learn about individual space or equine communication. A home-raised foal is often treated as a pet, given titbits and cuddled, giving him the idea that he can 'buddy up' to people. This may be fine with a little foal, but is not nearly so much fun with a rowdy three-year-old!

The foal is brought into a stable at night and turned out into a featureless paddock during the day, so he has no opportunity to learn by exploring. Physically, there are few challenges in most fields – no streams to negotiate, no banks to jump up – so his physical development is minimal.

At six months, or even younger, the foal is suddenly taken away from his mother and his diet is changed from milk and grass to concentrated feed. This is very traumatic. Naturally, weaning is a gradual process that happens between 9 and 18 months, and colts and fillies often remain in the same group as their mothers for three or four years. Once weaned, the domestic foal is often kept for two or three years doing very little to develop either physically or mentally, until it is time to start riding him, at which point everything happens at once.

So, we can see that even within the first six months we have set up the possibility of problems in the future, and certainly not laid the foundations for the mental and physical development that will maximize the horse's ability to perform in later life.

This description of early life is not the experience of all horses. For some, such as those in the racing industry, life is even less natural. For others, such as native ponies raised on the moors, mountains and plains, life is more natural. Horses raised in intensive

conditions are often sheltered from experiences because people believe they may hurt themselves. This overprotection means that they have little opportunity to learn about other horses and the outside world, and they actually become more of a risk to themselves and others. Horses that have the opportunity to learn and explore will do so gradually, and they are better equipped to cope both with their lives as members of a society of horses and with the demands of humans.

However, we must not be too hard on ourselves. Most of us have to keep our horses in locations and systems to which there are no immediate alternatives. If you only have one mare and you want to breed from her, it is very difficult to find stallions that are socialized to run with mares instead of covering in hand. Nor do you have the option of run-ning the mare and foal with a band of horses. In the wider picture, you will probably not have a choice about the type of grazing to which your horse has access; if he is boarded at a livery yard, you have to accept the yard set-up.

Nevertheless, by looking at how our horses' lives diverge from their natural lives, we can come to understand why they behave as they do and take steps to remedy any problem where possible. Over time, we can work to change the cultures and regimes that we impose on horses, so that horse-friendly systems become the norm.

### ■ Socialization
The bay mare is 14 years old and has never had, or lived with, a foal. She was intensely interested in the new baby and spent the day following the mare and foal around. We can understand why some mares have problems accepting their foals when we realize that they may never have seen a foal before giving birth.

# Beyond the Basics

Once we can fulfil the psychological needs of our horses, we have a strong base for success. However, human involvement can lead to other problems, resulting in behaviour that both we and the horse find it difficult to cope with. Often, it is a combination of factors that interact to cause problems for the horse.

## Physical Pain

An animal that is in pain is under stress. It is the same for horses as for humans, yet humans can take an aspirin or visit the doctor – horses can't. Undiagnosed illness, or pain due to tack, old injuries and/or insensitive riding may all trigger behavioural problems. There are horses that behave perfectly well except when doing a specific activity: this may be due to discomfort associated with the action of the bit, for example, or the rider's position in the saddle. Some horses simply cannot physically perform what is being asked of them.

We often presume that horses don't do what we want because they are being pig-headed. However:

❍ A pony that refuses to jump may be continually forced to do so with no consideration for the fact that he may have undetected unsoundness.
❍ A horse that refuses to load may actually find the strain of travelling very uncomfortable.
❍ A horse that is difficult to shoe may find the position in which the farrier holds his leg painful.

These are causes of behavioural problems that humans would find difficult to identify, but we must be aware of them as we try to understand why our horses do what they do. In fact, we must understand such behaviours as communication. There is no clearer way for a horse to say that he has a problem than by refusing to do something.

## Confusion

Most people do not understand how animals (including ourselves) learn. In addition, we often do not realize that our bodies give out signals that horses pick up. We use punishment inappropriately and fail to read the messages a horse is giving us.

### Individual Personality

Horses have varying personalities that are the result of inheritance and experience. We need to approach every horse as an individual and recognize that a technique that works for one horse may not do so for another. For example:

❍ A nervous horse will respond to harsh handling by becoming panicky, while a more assertive character may become aggressive.
❍ A horse that has strong opinions about what he wants to do may react badly if a handler tries to force an even stronger opinion on him, but will respond positively to gentle persuasion.
❍ A horse that is timid may appreciate a confident handler who leads the way, while a confident horse may be suitable for a nervous rider.

We can begin to understand a horse's personality by observing how he behaves. We can then try to find effective techniques to use when working with that particular horse.

■ **Confusing messages**
What is this horse going to understand, when the rider's legs are saying 'go' while the reins say 'stop'?

Confusion arising in training is a major cause of behavioural problems. A horse has to understand what is being asked of him in order to be able to carry out the request. If he doesn't know what is wanted, and no one tells him when he has done the right thing, how will he ever learn?

A horse that finds humans confusing will begin to expect the worst. He may become difficult to handle, or he may just switch off and ignore us. It is important that we take everything step by step and make sure we are doing our bit as teachers, instead of blaming horses for not learning what we want them to learn.

## Bad Experiences

Horses have strong, long-lasting memories of bad experiences, particularly of the place where something happened or the person involved. This is an obvious survival trait: if a predator jumped out from behind a certain bush, the place where that happened is going to be engraved on the horse's memory.

Horses can discriminate well. Some will remember a particular person who hurt them; others will recognize that they have always been abused by men, but will tolerate women; others will decide that all humans are potentially dangerous. The way a horse responds to a bad experience will depend on the horse and the situation. A rider who makes a mistake when jumping may be forgiven if rider and horse have a good relationship, built on trust; a rider who gets on an inexperienced horse and frightens him may leave a long-lasting negative impression on the horse.

This ability of the horse to discriminate can help us because it means that, with care, we can change the horse's attitude from negative to positive. By changing the situation in which we try to do something, or altering the routine we follow, we can eventually produce the behaviour we require.

# Case Study: Kabbilah's First Year

Kabbilah was a nine-month-old Arab foal and his owner was finding his behaviour increasingly unmanageable. He was rowdy, and anyone entering his paddock was liable to be charged and jumped on. At my first visit, it was clear that he thought humans were of no consequence. He tried to nip constantly, putting on a halter was almost impossible because he kept grabbing it, and he had no idea about how to lead.

'Kabbilah had very limited contact with other horses… his turnout area was tiny and he was only outside for four hours a day .'

We looked first at his lifestyle. It was evident that Kabbilah had very limited contact with other horses, although a mare, Rosy, lived next door. His loosebox was bigger than average, but his turnout area was tiny and he was only outside for four hours a day. We decided to make some changes. He was given more time outside, and we made an opening in the partition between his box and Rosy's so that they could have physical contact with each other.

### ■ Kabbilah as a foal (above)
Kabbilah is playing with his mother in lieu of having any other companion. However, she does not give a clear signal that he should not do it but simply moves away, which becomes part of the game. She was the foal's only 'playmate', so it is not surprising that he tried the same behaviour on humans because it was all he had learned to do.

## One year later

Kabbilah, now a yearling, has been turned out with an unshod adult mare, with whom he is friends in the stable. Note the contrast in his approach. Rosy is giving signals to him to be careful and his curiosity is tempered by controlled caution.

Kabbilah approaches Rosy with great caution but she warns him not to crowd her. The two horses tentatively touch noses and exchange breath.

The two trot side by side, but Kabbilah still wants to approach and he sniffs Rosy's hind leg. A second later he bites her and she kicks him in the chest, just hard enough to ensure he does not repeat the action.

Rosy settles to graze. Kabbilah is still very interested in her but is wary after being kicked. Within five minutes the two have settled to graze side by side.

# Setting ground rules

Kabbilah's behaviour changed within a week. He calmed down and people could enter the paddock without drawing his attention. Having established that he couldn't climb through the gap between the stables, Kabbilah spent his time grooming with Rosy. When he bit her, she would either bite him back or move away, neither of which was a good outcome for him. As another improvement in his behaviour, we taught him to step back in the stable when someone wanted to enter. This was done by waving a plastic bag at him and saying the word 'Back'.

Next we decided to turn Kabbilah out with Rosy, to allow her to teach him about acceptable behaviour. Once the fencing had been made safe, Kabbilah was turned out alone in the big field for the first time, where he galloped around for 20 minutes. However, within a week he was spending time hanging around at the gate, looking for Rosy. Kabbilah was by now a yearling and had not been turned out with another horse since he was weaned at 8½ months. Despite this, turning them out together went smoothly enough. Kabbilah approached Rosy carefully – her body language

was so subtle that we couldn't spot how she was telling Kabbilah to keep his distance. At one point he bit her hind leg and she kicked him in the chest, but she was unshod and no harm was done.

Kabbilah's behaviour did improve, but not completely. He knew exactly what he could and couldn't do with Rosy, and what he could and couldn't do with people. We began to work on gaining his attention, making him keep his distance, teaching him not to bite and how to lead, all of which he learned and understood quickly. The plan for Kabbilah's second year is to build on the advances he has made. With a more natural lifestyle and careful education and training, we hope that he will have a successful racing career and one day become a breeding stallion who can actually run out with mares.

### ■ Learning about body space

I used a spinning rope to work with Kabbilah – the rope is stopped when he performs the desired behaviour.

The aim of this lesson was for Kabbilah to be attentive yet remain a metre or two away, rather than running on top of me or sidling up to bite.

Compared to Rosy's body language, the spinning rope is unsophisticated, but if used clearly it gets the message across. The colt can stop the spinning of the rope by doing what we want.

## Conclusions

Kabbilah has benefited from:

○ Having a companion with whom he can be in full contact.
○ More time spent outside to burn off energy.
○ Clear handling and training.

# 2 The Psychology of the Horse

*'Ridcully had never liked horses, animals which seemed to him to have only the weakest possible grip on sanity.'*
Lords and Ladies, *Terry Pratchett*

When we learn to ride, we are usually put on to a horse without the slightest introduction to how he 'works' — how he sees, hears and thinks. We treat him as though he were a car. We don't need to know how a car works: we just need to know how to work it. With horses, the two things are inseparable.

In our lives, we are constantly trying to understand other people's points of view. If human-to-human understanding is often difficult, how difficult is species-to-species understanding?

# How Horses Think

We can say that the dog's psychology is half-wolf, half-human. We still have some characteristics in common with dogs: we are predators, we live in dens, and we have strategies to make up with each other when we have fallen out. In evolutionary terms, horses are not like humans in their adaptation to the world. When domestic horses escape and live in the wild (as feral horses), they succeed admirably. It is worth bearing in mind that we are superfluous to the equine species: our paltry few thousand years of influence on 55 million years of evolution may have changed the way the horse looks, but we have barely scratched the surface of his psychology and physiology.

However, as mammals, we do share the majority of physiological reactions. Our brains and bodies work in the same way, although they are adapted for different lifestyles. And humans do have features in common with horses: both species have strong family bonds, we are gatherers of food as well as hunters, and we have ways of resolving disputes that involve subtle negotiation rather than domination.

We should be humble when making statements about how horses think. Many of the workings of the horse's brain are still a mystery to us. We can only interpret their thoughts from the way they behave, but behaviour is open to various interpretations. What we can say is that the horse's brain is extremely well developed for controlling physical movement. We also know that horses are born with certain behaviour 'pre-programmed' or instinctive. We see, too, that horses react emotionally to experiences: for example, a horse may become quite distraught when his friend leaves.

It is commonly thought that horses are poor at rational thinking, but we have to remember that rationality depends on one's perspective. What is rational in one situation may not be in another – it may seem rational to take a short cut across a piece of land, until someone tells you the land is mined. What is rational to us may not be rational to the horse. So, the rationality (to us) of going into a warm stable on a cold, windy night may be an irrational action to a horse. The horse's rationality tells

## Rational or Irrational?

I was in the process of starting (breaking in) a three-year-old Anglo-Arab colt. There was nowhere to turn him out, so I left him loose in the indoor school to burn off some excess energy. The horse spotted the large mirror that hung on the school wall. He pranced up to it, sniffed, squealed, and then spent half an hour play-fighting with his image in the mirror. He would touch noses with the 'other' horse, then the two of them would run their noses up the mirror together. Each time he tried to prance alongside his imaginary adversary, the other horse would vanish, so he would skid to a halt and double back in astonishment to look for himself. Even after numerous encounters, the colt did not work out that there was no other horse there. Finally, I covered the mirror to remove the distraction. Was this behaviour as irrational as it sounds? In the wild the colt would never have come across a mirror, but he would have come across other horses with which he would play or fight. He was simply responding to the visual signals that another horse was giving him.

him that enclosed spaces are dangerous, especially when you can't hear anything because of the wind.

On the other hand, so far there is no evidence that horses make elaborate plans based on thinking about the future. For example, many horses that dislike competing still willingly enter the horsebox each time, only to arrive at the show and refuse in the jumping ring. Human beings would refuse to get in the car in the first place. This is not to say that horses have no opinions and no ability to influence our behaviour, but they certainly do not appear to spend their time thinking up ways to outwit us, although some will learn how to do this if we give them the opportunity. So, if a horse succeeds in bursting out of the stable by barging past you, it is likely that he will try the same tactic again. However, it is doubtful that the horse spent time planning his escape – he simply took the opportunity, went for it and learned that it worked.

## Anthropomorphism

'Anthropomorphism' is the application of human attributes to an animal. Some people consider any form of anthropomorphism a sin; others treat their animals as people. Both approaches can cause problems for horses.

To increase equine well-being, we need to understand the differences and the similarities between horses and humans. So, as a simple example, to say that because I am cold my horse must be cold ignores the fact that horses tolerate cold much better than we do. This misconception leads us to dress our horses in rugs and keep them indoors, thus depriving them of their ability to control their own temperature and sometimes causing ill-health and behavioural problems. Conversely, our failure to recognize the similarities between horses and humans in the relationship between parents and offspring leads to foals being forcibly taken from their

■ **Safety in numbers**
These friends have chosen to stand in the same loosebox. Their close emotional ties mean that they are happy being physically close to each other. The door is always open, so they can leave whenever they want.

mothers in a manner that would rarely be tolerated with human children.

Anthropomorphism can be used when the evidence indicates similarities, but care must be taken not to decide what is best for the horse on the basis of what we would prefer for ourselves, thereby removing its ability to choose for itself. Of course, there are times when we do know what is best – for instance, in the case of a horse with laminitis that needs to be taken off grass – but we should not forget that we may have been responsible for the laminitis by overfeeding, another example of misplaced anthropomorphism.

# Talking 'Horse': Body Language

*lower lip droopy*

■ **Very relaxed, dozy**

*mouth clamped shut, lips tight*

■ **Tension**

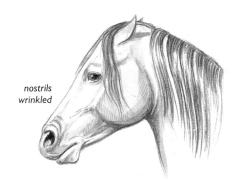

*nostrils wrinkled*

■ **Irritation**

*cleft above nostril*

■ **Pain, discomfort**

*long, wiggly top lip*

■ **Enjoyment of grooming/scratching**

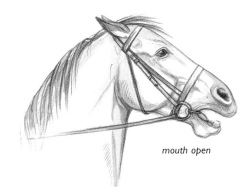

*mouth open*

■ **Discomfort from the bit**

■ **Licking and chewing**
Possible interpretations:
• Preparing to drink
• Relaxation after tension
• Stereotyped behaviour

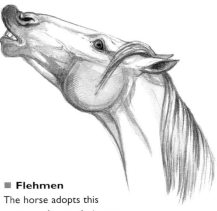

■ **Flehmen**
The horse adopts this posture when analyzing an unfamiliar smell or taste.

■ **Champing/mouthing/snapping**
A young horse will demonstrate this behaviour when approaching an older and/or aggressive horse.

**One ear forward, one ear back**
This indicates that the horse's attention is divided into two directions.

ears in 'neutral'

eyes may be half-closed

tail low

relaxed mouth, drooping lower lip

leg resting

**Relaxed**

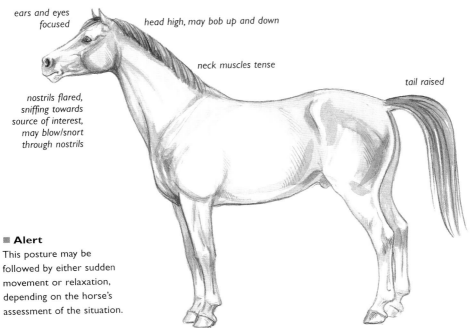

ears and eyes focused

head high, may bob up and down

neck muscles tense

tail raised

nostrils flared, sniffing towards source of interest, may blow/snort through nostrils

**Alert**
This posture may be followed by either sudden movement or relaxation, depending on the horse's assessment of the situation.

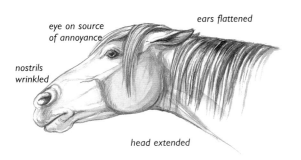

eye on source of annoyance

ears flattened

nostrils wrinkled

head extended

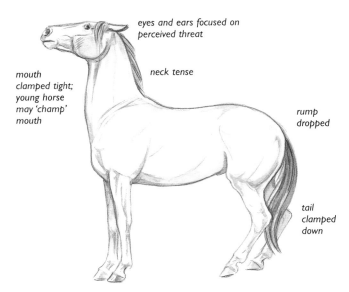

eyes and ears focused on perceived threat

mouth clamped tight; young horse may 'champ' mouth

neck tense

rump dropped

tail clamped down

### ▪ Head threat

The horse is indicating 'Go away' or 'Stay away from me'. This may be followed by a lunge and bite.

### ▪ Forward threat

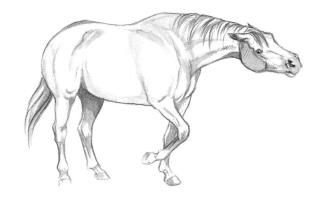

### ▪ Defensive and unable to run away

The hindquarters are turned in threat and the horse may kick if pressured further.

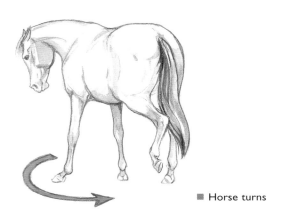

▪ Horse turns

### ▪ Aggressive kick threat (right and below)

This usually follows an ignored head threat.

▪ Horse reverses and swishes tail

▪ Horse kicks

### ■ Dropped head

Possible interpretations:

• Smelling – ears relaxed
• Stretching back and neck muscles due to tiredness – ears relaxed
• Stallion behaviour when driving other horses – ears flattened

### ■ Swinging head round

Possible interpretations:

• Removal of flies
• Threat to other horse/human to stay away
• Pain or irritation, eg from girth or colic

### ■ Tail swishing

Possible interpretations:

• Removal of flies
• Irritation with presence of person or horse
• Threat to kick
• Sign of discomfort, eg from spurs or colic

### ■ Pawing

• Clearing snow/moving food
• Investigating a smell
• Frustration

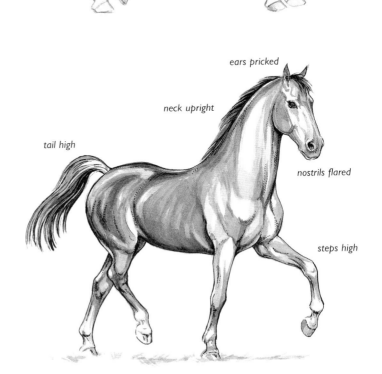

*ears pricked*

*neck upright*

*tail high*

*nostrils flared*

*steps high*

### ■ Excitement/play

# The Human Responsibility

Of the two species, horse and human, the onus is on us to understand the horse, not the other way round. Horses have not read books about horses, so they do not know that they are supposed to react to what we do in a certain way. A horse cannot second-guess us. For example, a horse that we are teaching to load does not know that our ultimate aim is to get him into the trailer. For all he knows, our aim may only be to get him to place a foot on the ramp, so by not achieving the ultimate aim on the first day we are not giving the horse the message that he has 'won'. It is unlikely that the horse has a conception of beating someone for the sake of being the winner. Once we accept this, we can stop saying things like

'He's deliberately doing that to annoy me.' The horse may not want to do something for whatever reason, but he is not trying to get one over on us for the sake of it.

If we are confusing to the horse, he will be confused. What he learns from us will be what we teach him, either intentionally or inadvertently. At no point can an untrained or badly trained horse say 'Ah, I know what this human wants, it's a shoulder-in.' The concept of the shoulder-in does not exist to a horse. We can see a horse fizzing with energy and say 'Ah, I know what this horse wants, he wants to go out and run.' We have the concept of another being having too much energy. This discrepancy between horse and human places us in a position of responsibility. It is likely that we have created the conditions that mean the horse has too much energy, so we need to give him an outlet for that energy. If we choose not to take up the responsibility and to blame the horse for being stupid, naughty or disobedient, we will not get the results we desire. Fortunately, horses are very forgiving – up to a point.

## Winning and Losing

I was trying to get a green horse to jump a 30cm (1ft) jump in the school. He kept ballooning over it and I narrowly stayed on board each time. By the end we were both nervous wrecks and making each other worse, to the extent that after 20 minutes neither of us wanted to get anywhere near what was now a pole on the ground.
I decided to abandon the exercise. A week later I set up a small jump in his field and, in a relaxed manner, we went back and forth over it with no problem. The horse had not got the idea that he had 'beaten' me the first time. He was simply afraid because I was making him nervous, and he was more than happy to jump in a different setting and different state of mind. I felt exactly the same way.

■ **'I know how to do this'**
The human has responsibility for communicating with the horse and teaching him what is required.

# The Heart of the Matter

The quotation at the beginning of this chapter represents a common interpretation of horse behaviour, but horses are not crazy. In certain situations they do react instinctively — their 'weak grip on sanity' is actually the flight reaction. For the horse, these apparently irrational reactions are essential. In the wild, if the undergrowth rustles the horse that stands around weighing up the danger will only do

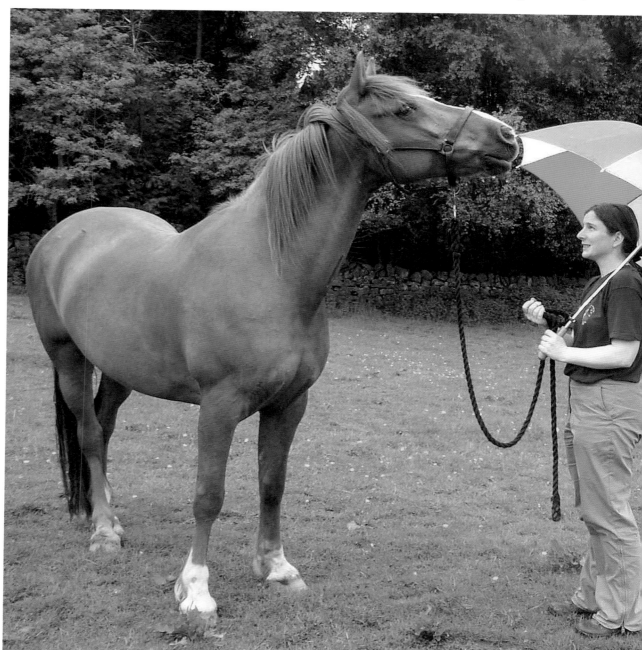

so once. It may just be the wind in the bushes – but it may be a lion.

Lord Byron described a horse as having 'The speed of thought...in his limbs.' The part of the horse's brain that controls physical movement is very well developed, and the result for humans is that in the time we have taken to register the threat, the horse has taken off.

## horse equation: scare = go

The process of training desensitizes the horse to all the scary things. A bombproof pony has learned not to find everything frightening. A good bullfighting horse has learned not to fear the bull. A good eventer has learned to overcome his fear of leaping into physical danger. The next time you are with a horse that is startled, take a moment to note how his heart is beating – you will feel the blood pounding through his body as adrenalin is pumped into his bloodstream to prepare him for flight.

A horse that is unable to run may well fight. Controlled by ropes and tack, he will throw himself around violently, barge his tormentors and run around in circles. In reality, the horse is not fighting: he is simply trying to flee. If freed, he will not turn and continue the battle, but will run away. If they cannot escape, some horses will defend themselves by kicking or biting, but they usually give numerous warnings that they are going to do so. Horses rarely attack, but if pushed too far occasionally will elect for fight rather than flight. I once met a woman who owned a Hanoverian stallion that had actually killed a man. This was in response to severe provocation: he had been tied up and beaten by three men and he suddenly snapped, attacking one of his persecutors. But this was a one-off – he was never aggressive towards his subsequent owner.

A horse that is truly terrified and cannot flee may seize up. This is a reaction we must be aware of, because it can be mistaken for the horse accepting what is happening to him. A horse that has frozen cannot move a muscle and trying to demand anything of him is useless.

■ **Desensitization**
An umbrella can be frightening, but giving the horse time and space allows his curiosity to overcome his natural desire to flee.

# Horse Time and Timing

Horses have a totally different concept of time to humans. A suspicious horse wants to spend so long satisfying his caution that we may think it verges on the ridiculous, because we know that the situation is safe. When working with a horse, especially a troubled or traumatized one, the time needed is as long as it takes – and that time is dictated by the *horse*. It may take a horse half an hour of examining the ramp of a horse-box before he will even put a foot on it. If we begin to push and hurry the horse, a battle will begin. If a horse needs re-starting and it takes six weeks to achieve each stage of the process, then six weeks is what is needed. What is right is what works to achieve the desired end *with the horse relaxed and accepting*. Some horses can be backed in a day, others may take months. That is horse time, and we can either accept it or buy a bicycle.

## Routines

The idea that horses need set management routines has been disproved by scientific studies. Horses that live freely vary the times at which they eat, sleep, rest and socialize because they respond to environmental changes. They will eat for most of the time, go to water when thirsty, sleep when the sun is warm and shelter when it rains – they may rest in the shade at the same time every day simply because the flies are active at that time.

The horse kicking the stable door at 7am in anticipation of his bucket is doing so because he has probably gone overnight without food and is very hungry, and/or is responding to the arrival of his owner. It is likely that horses become tuned in to human-created routines: for example, as autumn nights draw in and feeding time becomes associated with dawn and dusk. The behaviour is not due to the horse having a pre-programmed routine to which we must cater.

■ **Free to choose**
Horses at liberty can decide how to divide their time between eating, drinking, resting and socializing.

# Mood

Most owners would say that horses have moods. Taking time to watch them gives us the opportunity to compare their expressions and reactions at different times.

The weather seems to have a strong effect on the mood of horses. Prolonged rain makes my Welsh cob grumpy and he registers his annoyance with nostrils wrinkled and ears back as he shelters under a wall, being mean to his field companion. In hot countries, horses become active and high spirited if there is a sudden drop in temperature. We cannot know how a horse is feeling inside, so can only gain insight by trying to observe and understand the signals he gives out. We need to be sensitive – after all, it is not particularly pleasant being made to do things when you have a headache.

Mares and stallions are affected by their hormones. Some mares show great changes in mood throughout their menstrual cycle, others very little. Stallions' mood changes are more immediate, the effect of testosterone boiling up and subsiding quickly. A stallion may react to a stimulus such as being taken to a place where he has covered a mare, although a well brought-up stallion quickly calms down if he is told 'no' or his attention is diverted. In spring the 'sap' may rise in all horses. This is worth bearing in mind when starting to work with a young horse – autumn may be a better time of year.

■ **Energy to burn**
Horses express emotions as movement and this message is clear. We need to appreciate the subtler use of body language in order to understand our horses.

# 3 The Horse's Perception of the World

*'A horse has got two brains. He don't see the same thing out of both eyes at once. He's got a eye for each side.'*
Cities of the Plain, *Cormac McCarthy*

Horses receive information from the world in a different way to us. This means that they sometimes react in a way we don't understand and apparently for no reason. People often accuse horses of misbehaving because we presume they see, hear and feel in exactly the same way we do. In fact, not only do horses perceive the world differently to us, they interpret it differently too. If we can understand more about the way the horse experiences the world, we can understand more about the horse's reactions.

# Eyes and Vision

Horse lore says that it is possible to judge a horse's character by his eye, and some people have gone even further and taken up equine physiognomy, claiming to interpret personality from the physical features of the face. As applied to humans, this unscientific pursuit was discarded decades ago, so it seems odd to revive it with horses.

A horse's expression and demeanour will betray his emotions and his character as influenced by his emotions, but expressions and demeanours change, as do emotions. A horse that is constantly in a state of agitation may well have a wild expression, but this is an indication of the stress he is under, not the basic personality of the horse. As owners, we are often stuck with the horse we've got and we are happy with him: it does not help to be told the animal's shortcomings are set in stone. In fact, it is amazing to see the transformation that can take place in a horse's demeanour when he finds himself in a situation that is more comfortable for him. Even horses that have been on the verge of being shot because they were deemed dangerous can become calm and co-operative when treated properly.

The quotation reproduced at the start of this chapter is accurate to some extent. The horse's eyes are connected to separate sides of the brain, although there is some overlap. A horse can divide his attention between things on either side and this can be seen in the independent movement of the ears, which is the rider's or handler's best clue as to what the horse is actually looking at. A horse observing something new will assess the object with the side of his head that is nearer to the object, and will then turn his head and observe the object with the other eye and ear.

Because of this, horses have to be taught from both sides: for example, a horse that has only ever been handled from the left may try to keep humans on his left at all times (while a horse that has been mishandled from the left may try to keep humans on his right). The tradition of handling from the left side is a product of military tradition. If we want horses that are used to the scary things in the world, then we need to expose them to as much as possible. Leading, mounting and tacking up from both sides will help to achieve the objective of an adaptable, relaxed horse that can take everything in his stride.

## How the Horse Sees

What has science told us about the horse's vision that we need to keep in mind?

- The horse's visual field is almost 360 degrees.
- The horse has a blind spot at eye level that extends a short distance in front of him, so if you go to pat a horse between the eyes he cannot see your arm and hand.
- At ground level, the blind spot extends further, so a horse with his head up cannot see what is at his feet and immediately in front of him on the ground.
- The horse is long sighted.
- The horse has to move his head up and down in order to focus on objects close to him.
- The horse is very responsive to movement.
- The horse can see better at night than we can.
- The horse can see colour.

## The Visual Field

The horse's field of vision gives him the ability to see all around him, in order to check for danger and to see his companions at all times. The consequences for us are that:

❍ The horse will see things that we don't, and may react to them. This can take the form of running forward if something moves behind him.

❍ If we walk up to the horse in his blind spot, he may startle or back away. Stroking a horse on the nose and face is not the best approach, because the horse cannot see your hand. Allowing you into his blind spot is a sign that a horse trusts you.

❍ The horse needs to be able to drop his head in order to see what is in front of him, whether this is poles on the ground or a stony track.

**■ Field of vision**
By turning her head to one side, the horse is trying to bring the log into her field of vision.

❍ A horse can catch sight of the rider by raising his head and needs to be accustomed to this, otherwise he may suddenly panic.

❍ The rider's eye level is higher than the horse's, so you may be able to see over a hedge or wall and note that there is a cow in the field on the other side, while your horse may only see the top of a moving head and be justifiably cautious. Conversely, when leading a horse he may see things that you don't because his head is higher than yours, and he may respond accordingly.

❍ If a horse is being asked to negotiate an obstacle in his blind spot, he must be given the freedom to alter his visual field.

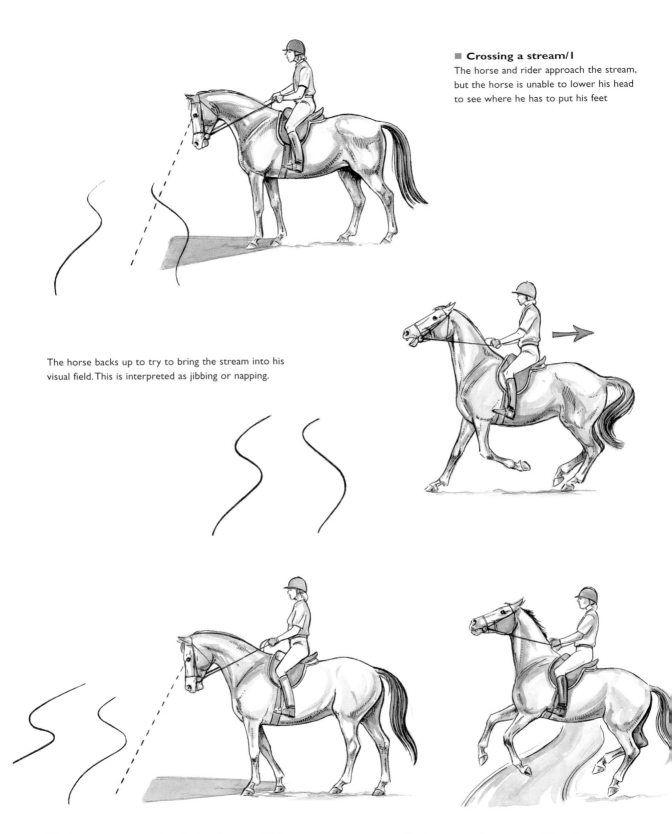

The horse and rider approach the stream, but the horse is unable to lower his head to see where he has to put his feet

The horse backs up to try to bring the stream into his visual field. This is interpreted as jibbing or napping.

The horse can now see where he is going to put his feet.

The horse may refuse to go or, if forced, may cat leap, which is uncomfortable for both horse rider. Escalation of force will only make the problem worse

■ **Crossing a stream/2**
The horse is free to examine the stream with eyes and nose. The rider needs to encourage the horse and not allow him to turn away.

The horse will continue to look and with his head down can raise his legs higher.

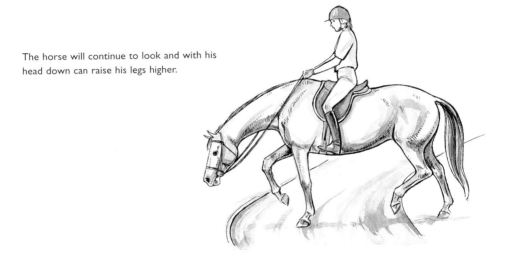

The horse may choose to jump but it will usually be a rounded leap. Grab a handful of mane and go with the movement.

# Detail

Horses' eyes do not focus in the same way as ours – that is, the lens of the eye is not the primary means of focusing. When we look at something, our eyes automatically focus without any conscious effort on our part. To study an object, a horse must be able to change the position of his eye by moving his head. This is similar to a long-sighted person moving a newspaper to arms' length in order to focus. Among other undesirable effects (see Chapter 10), riding with a firm contact on the bit prevents a horse from looking at objects properly and this leads to shying, jibbing and headshaking. Shying is actually the horse's way of bringing something into focus: if the horse is prevented from turning his head to see an object, he will swivel his whole body.

Just because a horse has been over the same piece of ground scores of times does not mean that he is being unreasonable if he reacts to something new. Horses are excellent at filtering out the familiar and spotting even the smallest changes, because in the wild any change in familiar surroundings can mean danger. A pile of pebbles washed on to the road by heavy rain caused my young horse to leap sideways into a (fortunately empty) road. I had not noticed the change.

Some horses will cope surprisingly well with new environments, such as town centres, where there is a clutter of unfamiliar objects. Perhaps this is because in this situation their filter mechanism is not switched on, or it may be that it is working overtime and there are just too many new things to which they could react.

## Light and Dark

Horses can see better in the dark than we can, which means they can be ridden in moonlight. Horses' eyes are designed to maximize the available light, which is not surprising considering that in their natural environment they live outside at night.

It is still not clear how quickly horses' eyes adapt to light and dark. As creatures of the outdoors, they do not need to accommodate sudden changes in light levels, but as they detect light better than we do they may be more affected by contrasts. Shadows on the road, dark stables and white objects can all produce reactions in the horse. Behaviour that may seem silly to us, such as shying at shadows, makes sense when we realize the horse is simply being careful not to put his hoof into what might be a hole.

## Colour

The scientific evidence about what colours horses see changes frequently. For our handling purposes, we can accept that horses see most colours and not worry too much about which ones. However, you should be aware that white objects often produce a strong reaction in horses.

## Movement

The horse's visual sensitivity to movement is obviously life-saving in the wild, but could be life-threatening when the horse is being ridden. The sudden movement of leaves may be a predator, but if it is just the wind and you are riding on a main road the flight reaction is undesirable. A horse will pick out a sheep moving on a hillside and stop to study it for an apparently ridiculous length of time. The rider knows that the moving object is a sheep but the horse doesn't. Modern four-wheel-drive tractors are often more frightening to a horse than small, old tractors or articulated trucks. Apart from the noise and the size, the rapidly moving wheels of the tractor are at the horse's eye level.

Horses are excellent at communicating by reading each other's – and our – body movements.

They are very sensitive to tension, which has massive implications when handling them. Brusque, jerky movements upset them because horses only move jerkily when agitated and tense, or when playing at mock fear. Similarly, very slow movements mimic a stalking predator and may make horses suspicious. We need to move smoothly and confidently, and adjust the speed and quality of our movements to the way the horse reacts to us. A horse that jerks his head in response to our movements is telling us that our movements alarm him.

In the end, with regard to how and what horses see, we must give them the benefit of the doubt and allow them time to look. We can never know exactly what information they are receiving.

**■ Observing movement**
This stallion is focused on the distance. Horses are adapted to study any distant movement with great concentration.

# Ears, Hearing and Vocal Communication

Horses have very good hearing and will often pick up sounds that we don't. Their ears can rotate through almost 180 degrees and can move independently. They are also an important means of communication and one of the easiest elements of equine body language for us to understand. Not only do the ears rotate, but they can also move from pinned back flat to pricked forward, giving them a huge range of possibilities for expressing emotion. To understand what the ears are saying is a major step in understanding your horse. The ears will show you where the horse's attention is and how he is feeling, and can be used to read how the horse is going to react, which is incredibly useful in training.

The sensitivity of horses' ears has implications for their behaviour when we are working with them.

○ Horses pick up sounds long before we do. On hearing hoof beats around the corner, for example, a horse may stop to take in the sound better – it may seem as if the horse has stopped for no reason and, depending on the rider, this may be a punishable offence.

○ Sounds may be louder to horses, and they can pinpoint the source of a sound more accurately than we can. This means that there are certain places where a horse may respond more to a sound than he would do in other places. Along a stretch of road bordered by steep hills, for example, the sound of traffic is amplified, so although the traffic is the same the horse is more disturbed by the volume of the noise.

○ Certain sounds bother horses more than others. Higher pitches seem to disturb them, so that a strimmer sometimes has more effect than a lawnmower. A horse will often jerk his head when disturbed by sudden loud noises.

The amount of vocal communication between horses depends on the situation. It is likely that we

■ **Locating a disturbance**
This horse has been startled and is listening to a noise behind him while preparing to run. Once he is calm, he will stop and turn to look at the cause of his alarm.

do not hear all their sounds. Some horse sounds are used as clear signals to other horses, and sometimes to us. For example, a whinny is a contact call, while a squeal is often a warning to another horse that his behaviour is not appreciated.

Some noises that horses make are not active attempts to communicate. For example, a gentle nose-blowing snort is given by a relaxed horse, but he is not intentionally trying to say 'I am relaxed.' However, we, and probably other horses, understand this to be a sign of relaxation.

Horses can learn individual words from us and also to respond to certain sounds when these auditory signals are given clearly and consistently. The unceasing chatting and clicking that some people carry out (almost without knowing they are doing it) is of no benefit in training a horse. 'Who's a lovely boy then, do you want a mint, look what a mess you've made of your bed, now just move over there so Mummy can put your hoof oil on' – this type of dialogue makes the horse ignore us, and may even irritate him.

We must not forget that a horse will only understand a word that he has actually been taught, and

## Windy Weather

Some horses are more excitable on windy days. The wind has several effects on a horse's hearing:

❑ The wind itself is noisy.
❑ It makes it difficult to distinguish where a sound is coming from and to distinguish one sound from another.
❑ It brings sounds to the horse from further away.

The wind also makes everything move, and this is probably quite disorienting for an animal that is sensitive to movement.

even then the word must be delivered consistently. Changes in stress and tone, according to the emotion of the speaker, will transform the word into a different sound altogether. There is little doubt that horses can learn to respond to words. However, it is also possible that in some cases the horse is not responding to the word itself but is actually reading the minute changes in body language that we make as we speak. Body language and visual cues may be more meaningful as instructions.

# Touch

This great big animal that will tolerate wearing heavy harness and weather temperatures of well below freezing has skin that can detect a fly landing on it. Of all the senses, touch is the one that we ignore most, yet it is the one that has the greatest effect on our horses.

Touch is important to horses. A foal will maintain physical contact with his mother when they run together, and horses mutually groom each other. When feeling insecure, my gelding will occasionally touch me with his muzzle. Friends will also put their heads over each other's backs, something that helps us in the process of backing a horse: if a horse thinks you are his friend, he will not mind you being there.

## Skin and Hair

The horse's skin is very sensitive and the degree of sensitivity varies between horses (chestnuts often appear to have quite sensitive skin), so we need to be aware of this.

As with us, parts of the horse's body differ in sensitivity. This must be remembered when grooming a horse, and the best way to find out which parts are more sensitive is to watch the horse's reaction to being groomed. If the horse fidgets, swishes his tail, tries to move away, cow kicks, looks back at you with an expression of discomfort or even turns to nip you, then he is not enjoying the experience.

We often expect horses to tolerate something that we would not. For example, using a coarse brush on the face or underbelly may tickle or hurt the horse. Although at times mud may be so caked that a softer brush will not shift it, it is worth bearing in mind that the only parts that really need to be spotless are those that go under tack. Obviously there will be times when the animal just has to grin and bear something, but if we care about our horses we must listen to what they are trying to tell us.

The horse protects himself from rain and cold with a layer of mud that becomes trapped as dust by the natural grease in the coat. The coat stands up when the horse is cold, and the horse sweats when he gets hot. Clipping and rugging destroy this natural thermal regulation, and also diminish the ability of the horse to synthesize vitamin D from sunlight via the skin. Putting more rugs on a horse to encourage him to lose his winter coat is not effective: it is the balance between daylight and darkness that influences coat loss after winter.

The mane and forelock insulate the horse, protect against flies, channel rain over and off the eyes, and aid communication by exaggerating movements.

## A Touching Moment

One of the most moving moments I have seen with horses was between two stallions. They were kept in looseboxes next to each other; the walls were about 2m (6ft) high and above the walls were bars. One stallion returned to his box after he had been turned out alone. He immediately rushed up to the bars where his neighbour was waiting, lifted his head and the two of them pressed their muzzles together and knickered madly. They were desperate for contact even though all they could touch was that small area of skin. Although they could sniff through the bars and see other horses, the stallions were permanently denied full contact with other horses.

Mane pulling and hogging are expressions of human vanity and make the horse more susceptible to insect attacks. Horses that resist having their manes pulled are labelled 'difficult', but it is not surprising that some object. After all, we do not go to the hairdresser to have our hair torn out. In terms of training, having plenty of mane is to be recommended because at times a chunk of mane in the hand is the only physical link between rider and horse (and may prevent you from grabbing the horse's mouth)!

A much more serious action is that of removing the whiskers from the muzzle. The horse's whiskers are extremely important because they are attached to nerves. The whiskers fulfil the role of eyes, because the horse cannot see what is at his muzzle. When faced with an electric fence for the first time, my horse was overcome with curiosity. While the older, wiser horses got on with grazing, he crept up to the fence, tentatively reached out, and touched the white tape with his whiskers. The reaction to the shock was tremendous. Half an hour later he was still prancing up and down the field trying to warn the others about the danger, but they ignored him.

The whiskers should never be removed. We would not remove a cat's whiskers, so why should we do it to horses? A comparison for us would be the loss of feeling in the tip of a burnt finger.

■ **Pleasant touch**
Although headshy, this pony trusts his owner and seeks out physical contact.

---

> **The horse uses its mouth for:**
> 1 Eating and drinking.
> 2 Investigating.
> 3 Communicating through touch and calling.
> 4 Grooming.
> 5 Fighting.

## The Active Mouth

We use the horse's mouth to control his movements, but at the same time we discourage the horse from using his mouth in the way he wants to.

The horse's mouth is his hand. He has a mobile upper lip, which he uses to search for food. The skin around the mouth is very soft and extremely sensitive – a horse that has to deal with rough grazing may develop a thick moustache to protect the lip.

Nuzzling, nibbling, nipping and biting are all on the same continuum for the horse. They have no moral connotations: a horse does not know that biting is wrong – he has to be taught. A horse that has been brought up with other horses will have learned this. If he bites an adult too hard, he will get a bad reaction! As trainers, we can do the same. It may be appealing when a foal nuzzles and nibbles you, but it is also the best time to lay the ground rules about what is acceptable. Colts may become increasingly mouthy as they get older. The problem of biting is dealt with in Chapter 9.

In addition to the various calls a horse makes, the

mouth betrays his emotional state and is the best indicator of relaxation or lack of it (see page 24).

## Human Touch

A horse that is handled roughly or in a manner that causes pain will become desensitized to human touch. Patting is in effect slapping and horses will tolerate it, but gentle stroking is more pleasurable.

It has been said that horses are 'into pressure' animals – that is, they push against pressure. In reality, horses react to pressure in the same way as other animals, including ourselves. If a friend takes your arm gently, you will probably move with him; if a stranger grabs your arm and pulls, you will resist. A horse will

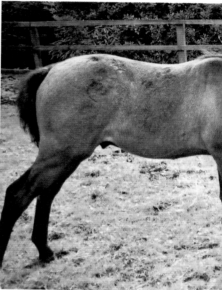

react against pressure when he is tense and when pressure causes pain. He will also resist pressure if he does not understand what the pressure means. When someone takes your arm, you understand that the action means 'Come with me'; an untouched foal does not understand that pressure on the headcollar means 'Come with me' and may pull back, rear or even throw himself over backwards to escape it.

Occasionally, a horse may simply not want to do what we ask, so we have to make it rewarding for him to do so. As in all training, we must constantly seek relaxation and understanding. Using the lightest pressure possible is the way to produce a sensitive, responsive horse.

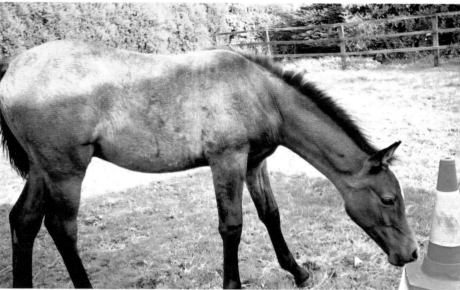

### ■ The horse's use of his senses

The foal Kabbilah uses sight, smell and hearing from a distance to investigate this new object.

Initially, he is startled and ready to flee. With a rider on board this would be called jibbing.

At full stretch, Kabbilah uses his nose and whiskers for further investigation while keeping the cone in view and being ready to run.

He then uses his lips to gather more information.

Finally, he uses his teeth. The foal cannot see what he is biting, so will only do so once he was satisfied his visual curiosity.

When the cone falls Kabbilah is startled, but confident enough not to run away. He returns to visual examination.

# Smell

We underestimate the importance of smell to the horse. When alarmed by something, a horse will sniff towards it with his nostrils flared. Horses show 'flehmen' when analysing a new smell: they raise their heads and curl up the top lip to trap the smell in an organ in their nose (see page 24). This is not a horse's way of laughing!

**■ Whiskers first**
The pony responds to calm body language by making contact through smell and touch.

Smell is an important means of communication and has other practical uses:

- Horses greet each other by exchanging breath and receive information from each other's scent.
- Horses will track other horses in the way that dogs track prey – droppings provide a horse with information about other horses.
- A stallion that is allowed to learn about mares will respond appropriately to a mare's hormonal state and will know when she is and is not in season.
- Horses use smell in choosing food and searching for water.
- Some horses become alarmed by unusual smells – for example, the aroma of pigs.

## The Smell of Fear?

Horse experts often warn us about the horse's ability to smell when we are afraid and to take advantage of that fear. So, if being afraid weren't enough, you can now be afraid of being afraid!

Animals, including humans, do produce smells when frightened. Horses in this state produce acrid sweat and droppings, and the biological effect of the smell is to make other horses wary – it is *not* the case that horses 'take advantage' of a frightened horse. When handling a horse, it is highly unlikely that your nervous state is detectable by smell, unless you are utterly terrified. It is more likely that horses detect tension in human beings from our body movements, and it is this that puts them on edge. This is good news, because it means that we can learn to control our movements through breathing and relaxation, and stop worrying about some mystical 'smell of fear' that may lead to our downfall as equestrians.

# Taste

Horses use taste as well as smell to distinguish foods. The horse's natural diet includes grasses, herbs, wild plants, leaves, fruits, wood, bark and even mud, and he needs to be able to distinguish between what is and is not good to eat. Horses seem to have a natural ability to avoid poisonous plants, but this varies from horse to horse and may not extend to unfamiliar plants. A new taste will produce head-nodding while chewing, followed by a flehmen reaction.

Some horses are fussy about drinking water, particularly if it is chlorinated. My cob avoids drinking from a bucket unless there is a good coating of green slime on the inside, even though it contains spring water. He prefers running spring water served in a trough.

# Exercise: Doing Less with Horses

We humans are sometimes uncomfortable to be around. We talk at our horses all the time and touch and fuss them for no reason. This exercise is a way of being more 'horse-like' around horses. By doing less, the horse will pay attention when you do ask him to do something, because your message is clear and the action is rewarded immediately.

1 When the horses are loose, whether in a yard, field or manège, go to see them.
2 Walk around and between them without saying anything or touching them.
3 Leave them.
4 Next time, do the same but sit a little way away from them, out of harm's way (perhaps on the fence). When they approach you, do not say or do anything. Let them sniff you and move away.
5 Go and catch your horse without saying anything. Do not do anything other than put on the headcollar and lead him to where you want to tie him – no patting or fussing.
6 Practise grooming and tacking up without saying anything and without doing more than is purely functional. Give the horse instructions only when necessary and praise the horse only when he responds to something you have requested.
7 Note whether the horses become more interested in you, the less you do and say. Do they seem to be more relaxed when you arrive? Do they take notice when you finally do say something?

# 4 Horse Keeping: Free Range or Factory Farm?

*'On occasion, glancing at the sleepy faces of its citizens,*
*It would dream of how it used to frolic in the meadows,*
*Of the clear blue sky, of spring water.'*
Caligula's Horse, *Rudolph Marku, translated by Dr Robert Elsie*

In Chapter 1 we considered the three elements that horses need in order to
be mentally balanced:

**1** Time for foraging    **2** Social contact    **3** Space to move

Many people are afraid to leave their horses outside, but overprotection by
restricting them can actually lead to suffering and make horses more liable to
be hurt or to hurt themselves. Many horses are kept as prisoners, confined in a
tiny space with minimal stimulation, no social contact and little exercise.

# How do Horses Organize Their Lives?

Feral horses are descended from domestic horses and have gone back to the wild, such as the mustangs of the USA or the brumbies of Australia. Studying feral horses allows us to challenge many of the assumptions that we have about domestic horses, because we can see that our horses would act in the same way if we vanished overnight. If we give our horses choices, they will tell us what they want.

### ■ Peace of mind

What's good for the horse is good for the owner. If we provide horses with access to shelter, food, water and companionship, they can look after themselves for much of the time, releasing us from tending to their every need, or paying someone else to.

On average, a horse spends his time as follows:

| | |
|---|---|
| Eating | 60 per cent |
| Standing | 20 per cent |
| Lying down | 10 per cent |

The rest may be spent interacting with other horses, moving around, looking at things and drinking.

In an intensive system, the time a horse spends just standing goes up to 65 per cent and the time he spends eating goes down to 15 per cent. It is easy to see that this leads to difficulties for the horse. Imagine if we were suddenly told we had to eat for 60 per cent of our time – it would not take long before we began to feel less than well.

# Effects of Restriction

| Behaviour | Restriction | Consequence |
|---|---|---|
| **Foraging** | Stabling | Horse cannot spend time searching and eating |
| | Feeding concentrated feed | Horse spends less time eating<br>Horse has too much energy<br>Digestive problems – horses are adapted to digest fibre, not cereals |
| | Haynets/hayracks | Horse not feeding in the natural position with his head down |
| | Keeping in overnight | Horse without feed for many hours |
| | Inedible bedding | Horse has nothing to occupy his mouth |
| **Social life** | Foals raised out of family groups | Young horses do not understand body space and body language |
| | Keeping horses in single sex groups (eg separating mares and geldings) | Horses do not learn to interact with others so must always be kept apart |
| | Separating the foal from his mother at six months or earlier | Trauma may lead to the foal developing abnormal behaviour<br>Sudden dietary change for the foal<br>Stressful for the mare |
| | Breeding in-hand | No normal courtship<br>Forced mating traumatic to the mare<br>Possible pathological behaviour in the stallion |
| | Buying and selling horses | Disruption of family and pair bonds |
| | Isolating horses in looseboxes or at turnout | Horses cannot indulge in physical contact or even see other horses all the time |
| **Movement** | Keeping horses inside | Horses stationary for many hours<br>No room to roll<br>No time playing to develop physically |
| | Overstocking | Horses have no room to move away from each other<br>Increased aggression |
| | Restricting food or water (eg piles of hay in the paddock) | Horses cannot spread out to their personal space<br>Increased aggression |
| | Limited exercise | Behavioural problems in horses with too much energy<br>Physical problems due to lack of exercise |

# Feeding

Horses fed meals at regular intervals generally eat all the available food in one go. Horses with constant access to food eat some, then rest for a bit, then eat some more.

The question all horse keepers must address is: what exactly is my stabled horse going to *do* between finishing his food at, say, 7pm and my arrival at 7am the following day? During that time, not only is the animal unable to fulfil any of his natural behaviours other than resting, but he also goes without food for about 12 hours, which is completely unnatural and causes discomfort, perhaps even suffering.

So, if we are to insist on our horses being shut in overnight, we have to address this issue. A large amount of forage, an edible bed or a top-up late at night are three improvements, but we also need to ask ourselves whether it is really necessary to shut horses in every night. The door-kicking and high activity levels seen first thing in the morning are not because the horse has just woken up but because he is very hungry and completely fed up. This stress may be further enhanced if individual owners in a livery yard feed their horses at different times. In this situation, some horses are fed early while others have to wait until their owners arrive, watching the luckier ones being fed. The contrast between relaxed grass-kept horses and frantic stable-kept horses is clear to see.

## The Grass-Kept Horse

People often think that horses cannot work off grass, but in fact they are designed to live on high-fibre

■ **Foraging**
This group of Furioso mares, foals and youngstock are digging for roots. During bad weather these horses are loose-housed in the buildings in the background, where they have forage, shelter and access to the outside.

diets of low nutritional value. Manufactured concentrated feeds contain high levels of sugars and proteins, and low levels of fibre. There is evidence that sometimes such feeds exacerbate behavioural problems because they give a 'sugar high' that increases aggression. The fact that horses can work off grass is demonstrated by horses living ferally, which eat food of poor nutritional value and travel huge distances.

In contrast, a horse on lush pasture 24 hours a day will not be particularly dynamic and may be prone to obesity and laminitis, but this can be worked around:

❍ If necessary, restrict grazing using an electric fence, although so-called 'starvation paddocks' are not ideal. Restricted grazing can make the horse frantic about food, may push him to eat rank grass or poisonous plants and, according to recent research, short grass may possibly be one trigger for laminitis due to high levels of certain sugars at particular times.

### ■ A natural environment
This Akhal Teke yearling lives in a group in the horses' natural environment of the Hungarian plains. The grazing is of low quality and is made up of a variety of plants, not just grass.

❍ To avoid a horse being sluggish, bring him in from the field for an hour or so before exercise. He will usually have a nap and, once he feels less full, be more active.

❍ Plenty of exercise is the best way to get a horse slim and fit and to stave off laminitis, but most people do not have two or three hours a day to ride. However, if you can find time for longer rides occasionally, do not worry that your horse will become tired – after an hour, a fit and healthy horse will only just have warmed up.

In the long term, we need to reseed pastures with grasses and plants that are more suitable for horses. Such seed mixtures are now available, including some suitable for laminitics.

# Social Groups

A breeding group of free-living horses consists of two or three mares, their offspring of the last three years and one or two stallions. Non-breeding groups may range from a pair of juveniles who have left the family to a number of bachelor stallions. At times, different groups (including stallions) may mingle — for example, to shelter together in winter. Occasionally, old stallions may be alone for a time, but they always try to link up with other horses.

Family and friendship bonds are strong. Mares often have a close bond with one another and are sometimes quite jealous, even objecting to the stallion showing attention to a friend. The bond between a mare and a stallion may also be strong, the mare rejecting other stallions that come on the scene. Stallions in the wild have been seen rejecting unknown mares that approach the group, and this behaviour is also observed in free-living domestic horses. Although groups change, mares in the wild often have friendships that last for many years, and it is likely that any changes involve gradual transitions — that is, horses will not usually be severed from everyone they know at one time.

A stallion's affiliation to his offspring extends to step-children. Once the young have left the group, aged two to four, the stallion will 'remember' those he has raised and will play with his sons if he comes into contact with them. He will also refuse to mate with daughters and step-daughters. However, this memory seems to fade if he does not see them for around 18 months.

Familiarity and time spent together are important factors in social organization and will reduce conflict and aggression. This is often not the case with domestic horses, where our systems actually encourage conflict:

## The Solitary Horse

If you have no option but to keep your horse on his own, there are ways to give him company:

❍ Spend time with your horse grooming, going for walks to graze or just sitting in the field.

❍ Go for rides with other people so that your horse has friends that he sees regularly.

❍ Keep him where he can see other horses in neighbouring fields.

❍ Graze him with sheep or cows to give him a feeling of herd security, or get one of these animals as a companion for him.

Long term, it is only fair to get a companion for your horse, but bear in mind that even a little pony can bring extra effort and expense, especially if overfed and underworked.

# Movement

The distance that feral horses move depends on the terrain and the season. If food is plentiful, they will not need to range over a large area in order to find it; when water is difficult to come by, they will travel long distances to drink. One thing is certain: horses at liberty move constantly, because they move as they graze. The horse standing motionless in a stable for 65 per cent of his time is doing something for which his body is simply not designed.

When young horses play they develop skills that will be useful to us – for example, rearing develops muscles that will be used in jumping. Again, a young horse standing in the stable is doing nothing to improve his strength and co-ordination, but is likely to be using his body in a way for which it was not designed, with the head up, weight displaced backwards and long periods spent stationary.

In nature, as horses get older they play less. Mares need to preserve their energy for rearing foals and stallions for keeping the group away from other stallions. (Stallions who become obsessive about this in the wild soon lose body condition, and actually decrease their chances of winning disputes and breeding.) It is possible that horses accused of being lazy may just be fulfilling their energy-preserving instincts. It is up to us to find positive ways to motivate them to move.

■ **Separation not isolation**
Despite the barrier, these horses are resting together and can touch. Turning out horses in isolation removes an essential part of their lives – interaction with others of their species.

○ The family group is not allowed to develop and stay together.

○ Constant buying, selling and shifting of horses between owners and yards breaks emotional bonds.

○ Just as the arrival or loss of a member in a wild group causes turbulence, so it does in domestic situations, but in this case the coming and going is more frequent, thus raising overall stress levels.

○ Horses are often physically isolated from each other, even when turned out – for example, they may be kept in individual paddocks – so they do not form full relationships. This is often done for their own protection, but in fact it actually *creates* the problem it is designed to avoid because horses that have been isolated are then unable to interact properly with other horses.

# Health

A more natural lifestyle has health benefits beyond those of state of mind:

○ Horses that are stiff and ageing will benefit hugely from being at liberty to move all the time.
○ The circulation of blood is promoted by movement and injuries heal faster with increased circulation.
○ Dust allergies and COPD (Chronic Obstructive Pulmonary Disease) are virtually non-existent in horses kept outside, unless there are unnaturally high levels of pollen around due to cash crops.
○ Horses that suffer from sweet itch will be bothered by midges, and flies are troublesome in hot weather, but a horse with the option of a shelter will choose to come in when he needs to. A horse that is able to escape the insects will have less chance of developing sweet itch in the first place because he will avoid being bitten. Midge-proof rugs are now available to enable horses with sweet itch to stay outdoors.
○ The horse's body itself manufactures vitamin D (essential for healthy bone formation and muscle function) and part of the process takes place due to the effect of sun on the skin. A horse that is kept constantly indoors and/or rugged may not generate sufficient vitamin D; providing it in the diet is an option, but care must be taken because too much vitamin D is toxic. It is very difficult to know exactly how much vitamin D is needed and how much is being provided for a given horse, so allowing natural manufacture is probably safer.
○ The horse's jaws are designed to work with the head at ground level, and in this position the teeth wear evenly (the wear itself being due to silica particles in the grass). Horses that eat unnatural feeds with their heads up are more prone to tooth problems.

So, instead of installing dust-extractor fans in stables, feeding anti-allergy feeds and making our horses' lives even more unnatural and expensive, let's look to the simple solutions.

## Head Down

The horse is designed to spend his time with his head at ground level, constantly shifting his weight from leg to leg. Among other benefits, this position increases blood circulation because the feet assist in pumping blood up the legs, stretches the back muscles and allows the horse to breathe with his airways fully open. Placing buckets and mangers at floor level and putting forage on the floor will increase the time the stabled horse spends in this position.

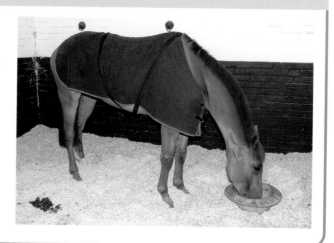

# Stable Set-Ups

It is said that the Emperor Caligula had a manger made of ivory for his horse. Sadly, he didn't do the horse (or the elephant) any favours. The design and routine of stable yards is often not conducive to a horse's peace of mind.

Naturally, a horse spends his time calmly grazing, occasionally raising his head to look around or when his attention is caught by a sound or movement. When observing ponies running free on moors, I am always struck by the silence. Any sound causes them to raise their heads and consider whether they need to take action.

In a yard, the environment is hyper-stimulating. There is constant coming and going of people and horses, food being delivered in small quantities and often a radio blaring. It is sometimes said that a busy yard prevents boredom in horses but, having observed a large yard over three weeks, day and night, I can safely say that it is periods of activity that wind the horses up and produce weaving, door-kicking and whinnying. When nothing was happening in the yard, the horses were resting peacefully.

■ **Invasion of body space**
Having been abused, this mare dislikes having people near her. There is not enough space in the loosebox for her to move away, so she is trying to warn off the photographer.

## Solutions

### Stabling

❍ Make looseboxes larger. A 4x4m (12x12ft) loosebox does not give a horse room to roll, walk around in a circle or get a safe distance away from his neighbours should he want to. A horse in a loosebox with other horses on each side is unable to be within his own personal space. Ideally, a horse should always have space to roll,

**■ American barn system**
These looseboxes are equivalent to prison cells. There is a limited view outside and the horses cannot look out properly. The situation is worsened by fitting anti-weaving bars. Once the horse has finished his food, his only option is to rest.

## This season I'll be wearing…

When we read an advertisement, catalogue or article telling us about the latest product for our horses, we need to consider who actually benefits. Most of the time it's the company selling the product or the person promoting it, not the horse. Often it is the owner, who wants the latest fashion. Understanding horses and what they really need will save you a lot of money, and benefit your horse.

kick his heels, stand on his hindlegs and walk a circle. Close friends will share a large box.

○ Give horses a view. American barn-style stabling allows them no escape from the yard activity and nothing to look at. Windows will help and research shows that stereotyped behaviour can be reduced if horses can see out more. Try to ensure that all horses can see other horses.

○ Don't isolate. Find some way to give every horse companionship. Stallions are often kept out of sight of all other horses, but this does not allow them to fulfil their natural function of watching the herd. A stallion can form friendships with another stallion or a gelding, or another species altogether. *However, you must take care, especially if a stallion has been isolated for most of his life, is showing pathological behaviour or if there are mares close by.*

- Put openings in partitions. Allow horses to have contact with and groom each other by not separating them completely from their neighbours. A removable board will allow you to separate horses if necessary.

- Turn over areas to horses. Think of how much space in the yard is not available to the horses. Swept yards with hanging baskets may be very satisfying to human eyes, but they could be made available for horses to wander in, thereby giving them additional time outside the stable and the opportunity to associate with other horses over stable doors.

- Try loose-housing. Instead of filling a barn with looseboxes, allow the horses to roam over the entire area. It is important not to overstock — standard looseboxes allow overstocking because horses are physically restrained. A loose-housing area can also be used as a schooling area and/or divided into pens if necessary.

- Make indoor pens. A large agricultural building can be partitioned into pens if horses need to be separated. This gives the horses more space than looseboxes, all-round views and the possibility of always seeing and perhaps interacting with other horses.

- Make outdoor pens. If stables are designed to look out of the yard rather than into it, each one can be designed with a suitably surfaced pen to enable the horse to be outside. Electric fencing is sufficient to divide up the area.

## Fields

- Choose suitable fields. Horses thrive on well-drained fields that have plants of low nutritional value. Sloping fields are good because they often have natural shelter and horses stay fit by climbing up and down hills. In flat areas of the country, fields with trees or hedges provide shelter. Lush pasture grown for dairy cattle is not ideal for

## Summer and Winter

Contrary to what many people believe, horses can cope perfectly well with winter weather, provided they can shelter from the wind and rain. Cold is not a problem for horses: the action of gut bacteria on their food gives them their own central heating. It is summer weather that causes problems.

Heat stress is a problem for horses when it is sunny, and also when they are rugged up and unable to sweat naturally. Flies and midges are a menace, and horses in the wild spend a lot of time avoiding them. However, because we believe that we are protecting our horses in winter by shutting them away from the bad weather, we often neglect to provide shelter in fields that horses can choose to use. So, on a hot, sunny day we leave our horses out before going to work, wishing we could be outside enjoying the sun, while they have no escape from the heat and insects. Sometimes, if it is nippy in the early morning, we may even put on a rug, without considering that by afternoon the weather will be baking. Horses choose to shelter in buildings at just such times. When it is windy and raining they prefer not to be cooped up in a stable, where they cannot hear danger and the roof creaks.

Horses control their temperature behaviourally, by moving to areas that are cooler or warmer, and physiologically, by sweating when they are hot and by the raising of coat hairs to trap warm air when they are cold. As we cannot judge what the temperature will be like over a day, or what the horses feel, it is better to provide them with the choice of whether to shelter or not and leave it to them.

**■ 'Free-range' livery yard**
This livery yard gives horses the choice to be inside or out. They can arrange their lives as they want and have the health benefits of constant movement, natural food and fresh air. Although they may not be as clean as horses kept in an intensive system, they are content, and this system saves both time and money. Care must be taken with horses whose desire for company overrides their need for physical comfort. A thin-coated horse sometimes prefers to stay outside with his tougher companions than to shelter and eat. In such a case, a compromise will need to be found – for example, using a waterproof sheet or ensuring that the horse gets extra food.

horses: the grass is too rich and cannot stand up to the pressure of metal shoes.

❍ Keep stocking rates low. Traditionally, the lore has been 0.8ha (2 acres) for the first horse and 0.4ha (1 acre) per horse for the rest. Depending on the ground and the amount of forage, often this is not enough: 0.8ha (2 acres) per horse would be more realistic. In the wild, as horse numbers increase, they spread out more. In domestication, it is the same: the more horses, the more the social pressures, and therefore the more ground that is needed. When there is plenty of grazing, horses can be kept in a smaller area.

❍ Open all the fields in winter. The tendency is to restrict access to land in winter to prevent poaching. In fact, if horses can roam over all available land, they will continue grazing all winter because grass keeps growing. Socially, they will feel less pressured by a lack of personal space and there

possible, with two entrances so that timid horses feel they can get out easily.

❍ Stone up gateways. Excavating a gateway and filling it with graded stone (ideally sandstone) prevents deep mud from forming and can help eliminate mudfever. Dumping building rubble into a quagmire is not a good idea.

❍ Install and maintain field drains. When we develop properties for horses, we tend to invest a lot in the stables and yards while ignoring the pasture. Installing good drainage in a field or areas of hard standing is an invaluable investment, although it is worth bearing in mind that breaking up soil disrupts the natural drainage.

will be less mud than on an intensively grazed paddock. Once rolled, harrowed and rested, land recovers amazingly quickly when spring comes and hay or haylage can still be made. If horses are still getting some nutrients from winter grazing, the winter feed bill will be reduced.

❍ Provide shelter. A horse knows better than we do when he needs shelter. Wind and rain are the problem for horses, not cold. High walls, hedges, trees and dips in the terrain are natural shelters; built shelters can be as simple as high wooden screens. Horses can be left to choose when to come into the yard or stables if the set-up allows. Field shelters need to be as large and open as

## Showing and Competing

The quickest way to give horses more natural lives would be for the competition, showing and breed societies to change their demands. At present:

❍ People are afraid to turn out their horses in case they get knocks or bumps, because they will be marked down.

❍ Show animals must have their manes pulled and whiskers shaved in order to win classes.

❍ Dressage competitions demand that certain types of bits are used and ban alternatives that are more humane.

❍ Owners are afraid of their horses growing thick coats, so rug them all year.

And so on. However, a good judge should be able to pick out a good horse even if he has a full mane and is ridden in a headcollar. If a horse is collected, he is collected, whether he has shoes on or not. The societies that govern the horse world have the power to change welfare for the better, should they choose to do so.

# Case Study: Lena

Lena is a 15-year-old ex-racehorse. Having finished racing, she was kept in the racing world to accompany strings of racehorses on the gallops. When her owner went to work away from home, Lena was left alone in a field without shelter, where she lost condition rapidly. In order to rescue her, a loan was agreed and Lena was moved to a traditional livery yard. She had company, but was kept in at night and turned out in a small paddock during the day. She weaved and box-walked when shut in the stable. In addition to being psychologically damaged, Lena had physical problems – not uncommon among racehorses, whose working lives begin before they are physically mature. She had problems with her stifle joints and her sacroiliac (the high point of the rump).

## Lifestyle change

Some of Lena's behaviour was unusual: for example, the rustling of cellophane would make her relax because she associated it with people relaxing to have a cigarette break. Other behaviour was typical of racehorses. Her mouth was damaged and pressure on the reins made her go faster, as did the rider's weight shifting forward in the saddle. This was a direct result of her training – it was what she had been taught.

Lena was afraid of everything. The world was worrying and, until proved safe, life was frightening. She was very defensive about food and would cross the yard to warn off any horse that might steal it. On one occasion she defended three haynets from two field companions, cantering backwards and forwards while not eating a mouthful.

After two years Lena was moved to a natural living system. She was kept outside in a group, with 24-hour access to shelter. Her new owner began working on her physical problems, using shiatsu massage and ground exercises. Her saddle was changed to one with flat panels that could be fitted to her. To overcome her discomfort with the bit, she was worked in a rope halter.

The natural life has transformed Lena. She has become calm for most of the time, although she is still liable to take fright. Her aggressive behaviour around food has virtually vanished: a pony that had previously been terrified of her now feels confident enough to be close to her while she eats.

Lena is still complicated. Her usual response to being approached is to wrinkle her nostrils and turn her head away, but if given space she will come up in her own time. If anything upsets her she will go rapidly from looking mildly concerned to full flight, and she responds to the 'go faster' cues as though she has never left the track. If confined in a stable, she will begin to weave. The main difficulty in her management is keeping the weight on her, but each winter this becomes less difficult. Her winter coat is becoming more weatherproof and she needs rugging only in times of prolonged wind and rain, when she chooses to stay outdoors with the other horses. She is fed a high-energy forage feed of grass nuts and unmolassed sugar beet, and feeding begins before she starts to lose condition.

Of course, it is impossible to give Lena back her early years, but she is much more peaceful, even if life is a little worrying – and sheep utterly terrifying.

## Conclusions

Lena has benefited from:

○ A settled herd life with lasting relationships.
○ Natural living conditions without competition for food.
○ Addressing physical problems.

# 5 Stress, Distress and Suffering

*'They wrecked the horse then. The horse went mad and didn't want to know anybody. The horse went stone mad.'*

*Keith Irving in* Pony Kids, *Perry Ogden*

What exactly is stress? Think about how you feel if you are about to jump a fence that is larger than normal – is your stomach churning? What you are feeling is an effect of stress. Stress is the body's response to unusual conditions that require a special reaction. It may be displayed physically – for example, by a person becoming lethargic due to dieting. It may be noticed psychologically – for example, feeling nervous in anticipation of a job interview.

Substances that affect behaviour and mood include hormones and neurotransmitter chemicals. Examples of hormones are testosterone and adrenalin; neurotransmitters include endorphins, seratonin and dopamine. When operating properly, the body's production of chemicals is in balance.

# How Do We Know When All is Not Well?

Problems arise when there is too much or too little of a given chemical over time. So, extra adrenalin is a great help for a short time when flight or fight may be needed, but production of adrenalin over a long period of time will make a person constantly ready for action and unable to relax. Endorphins give a sense of well-being; a large release of endorphins relieves pain but may also give the sensation of being high. Imbalances of endorphins and seratonin may lead to feelings of depression. Substances such as cocaine or heroin mimic such natural body chemicals and give unnatural highs and lows, sometimes leading to addiction. Horses' bodies function in the same way.

Being under stress does not necessarily mean that the horse is distressed and suffering, but stress does place strain on a horse and distress may result. Take the example of a stallion shut in a stable, who can see other horses but never has contact with them, and is overfed and underexercised. If he is only brought out to cover mares, he will have high levels of hormones associated with sexual arousal but no outlet for the resulting desires except when allowed to mate. This restriction can cause frustration, and raised levels of adrenalin and testosterone may make the animal aggressive and dangerous.

Behaviour is used to diagnose states of physical health – for example, we accept a horse that repeatedly looks at his sides may be suffering from colic. Similarly, behaviour is an indicator of emotional well-being. To recognize when a horse is showing signs of behavioural distress, we first need to consider what an unstressed horse is like.

A horse at peace is a relaxed animal whose description sounds like that of a dozy old plod – but it also applies to breeding racehorses or jumping ponies. The horse spends time grazing, mooching around, resting, sunbathing and contemplating the horizon. When there is cause, this horse is transformed. A sudden noise or the arrival of a strange horse will change him into a prancing, snorting beast. Once the source of excitement has passed, the horse returns to his relaxed self.

If we do not recognize our horses in the above description, it is because we are accustomed to seeing animals in some state of arousal. This may be manifest as constant alertness, agitation, excitement, nervousness or aggression, which are appropriate responses in certain situations. However, if the horse is not relaxed most of the time, we need to examine why. Conversely, horses should be reactive when necessary as well. A horse that shows no interest in what is going on may be depressed.

Behaviours that should lead to concern are those that are not found in horses in a natural context or those that are being applied in an unnatural way, as substitutes for normal behaviour. For

## Abnormal Behaviour

To reduce suffering in any animal, basic behavioural needs have to be met. I met a young Arab stallion that had been kept on his own for a number of years. Bayo was incapable of interacting with other horses but played games with himself, biting his own front legs and sniffing his sheath and squealing. When he was eventually turned out with a companion, he didn't know what to do and would run away from invitations to play. That need to play was so strong that Bayo had developed an abnormal way of doing it.

example, horses in the wild do not weave, but weaving is actually a modification of the natural behaviour of walking.

## 'It Doesn't Seem to Bother Him'

Unlike dogs, horses do not squeal when hurt. Owing to their social organization, they do not need to communicate to each other that they are hurt. Dogs' interactions sometimes involve them being bitten by other dogs, so they squeal to say 'That's too much.' If horses get into a dispute, one will simply get out of the way when he has had enough. Just because a horse accepts something does *not* mean that he is not suffering. A horse may

■ **Nervous fear**
This pony is frightened of people. With nowhere to run, his reaction is one of resignation but he makes no threat to kick. Notice how he is standing as far away from the photographer as possible and how tense and tight his mouth is. His ear indicates that his attention is on the photographer, but he is avoiding looking at her.

**■ Total relaxation**
This stallion delivering milk in Honduras is so relaxed he's almost horizontal. Note the relaxation of the rider and absence of a bit.

stay in a field with no water and die rather than jump out to find some.

A horse responds to pain by taking evasive action. Evasion is traditionally considered to be a sign of disobedience and we try to prevent it. However, we should instead be considering *why* the horse is taking evasive action – it is more likely to be discomfort than 'naughtiness'. If a horse is constantly prevented from making himself comfortable, he may close in on himself and become unresponsive. To say that something doesn't bother him does not mean that it doesn't. It just means that we can't recognize it.

## 'He Doesn't Know any Different'

Just because an animal has been kept in a certain way for his entire life does not mean that he is accustomed to his life. It is generally accepted that factory-farmed animals suffer, although they have always be kept under the same conditions. A horse that has never been allowed to be free in any area bigger than a loosebox may be alarmed when first turned into a field and want to come in. Strategies to make him more comfortable, such as fencing a smaller area to begin with and turning him out hungry so that he has an incentive to graze, will help. As he becomes accustomed to being outside, his behaviour will begin to become more normal.

# Stereotyped Behaviours

Some behaviours become habitual. They may occur in specific situations or become generalized, occurring whenever the horse is stressed. Box walking, weaving and crib-biting are classic examples. We know these as 'vices' and say they are caused by boredom, yet observation shows that horses exhibit these behaviours when there is activity in the yard, particularly at feeding time.

Scientific studies show that when performing a stereotyped behaviour a horse appears to be stimulating his brain to release chemicals that give pleasure, as a way of alleviating the stress he is under. (Interestingly, crib-biting has been found to lower heart rate, thereby having a calming effect.) The result is like drug addiction, in that the horse becomes dependent on the stress-relieving chemicals and may carry out the activity at times when there appears to be no significant cause of stress. The horse has found a way to make himself feel better, but – like humans – eventually comes to need the coping mechanism just to feel normal. There is also evidence that high-sugar diets exacerbate stereotyped behaviours.

■ **Distress**
This little stallion, tied up at a horse fair, is weaving because he is worried by the situation. There is activity all around him, which suggests that boredom is not the cause of his behaviour.

# Exercise: Symptoms of Stress and Distress

Many types of behaviour are simply natural behaviours that are used out of context or in a way that is inappropriate. For example, digging a hole in a stable bed by pawing is the natural behaviour that a horse uses when digging for roots or clearing snow. It is a normal activity directed to a new end. Similarly, rearing when ridden is a redirection of natural play, flight, fighting and mating behaviour.

Look at each of the behaviours in the list below and try to decide what natural behaviour (if any) it is a modification of. Is the behaviour associated with feeding, socializing or movement?

This list is not exhaustive. Animals are creative and individuals can come up with other behaviours: I once encountered a stallion that continuously banged his chin on the top of his door.

Although the occasional occurrence of a certain behaviour is nothing to worry about, it is important to ask why the horse did what he did. This will help us to avoid the situations that may lead to permanent establishment of the behaviour. For example, if a horse shows aggression to the handler because a lot of pressure is being applied and the horse cannot leave the situation, the pressure needs to be reduced; a horse that begins to grind his teeth during training is finding the activity difficult and may need a break or to go back a step.

Horses that have long-established behaviours may perform them as habits, rather than because they are under stress at that moment. For example, a horse that has developed the habit of chewing frantically on the bit may do so even when the rider's hands are gentle.

| Well recognized | Not always recognized | |
|---|---|---|
| Weaving | Constant movement – high activity level | Constant vigilance (eg straining over the stable door) |
| Box walking | | |
| Crib-biting and windsucking | Head bobbing | |
| | Aggression towards other horses | Constant or frantic lip licking or chewing |
| Kicking | | |
| Self-mutilation – biting his own sides | Tail swishing | Whinnying a lot |
| | Foot stamping | Listlessness |
| Rug biting and tearing | Pawing | Grinding the teeth |
| Aggression to humans | Door kicking | Excessive drinking |
| Bolting | Freezing | Lack of interest |
| | Headshaking | |

## 1 ATTENTION SEEKING

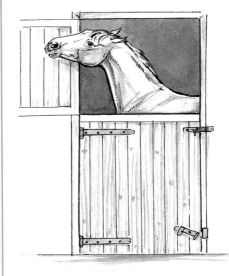

- **Face pulling**
- **Kicking stable door**
- **Leaning side to side**
- **Constant nudging and nipping**

## 2 DEPRESSION

- **Little interest in other horses or activity**
- **Standing for long periods**
- **Over-calm**
- **Lack of interest in food**

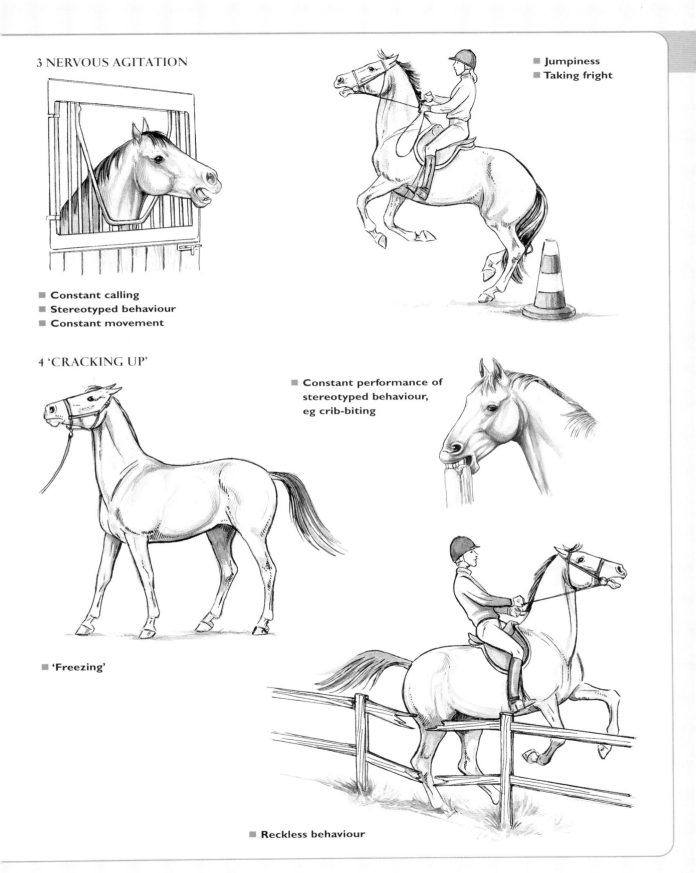

## 3 NERVOUS AGITATION

■ Jumpiness
■ Taking fright

■ **Constant calling**
■ **Stereotyped behaviour**
■ **Constant movement**

## 4 'CRACKING UP'

■ **Constant performance of stereotyped behaviour, eg crib-biting**

■ **'Freezing'**

■ **Reckless behaviour**

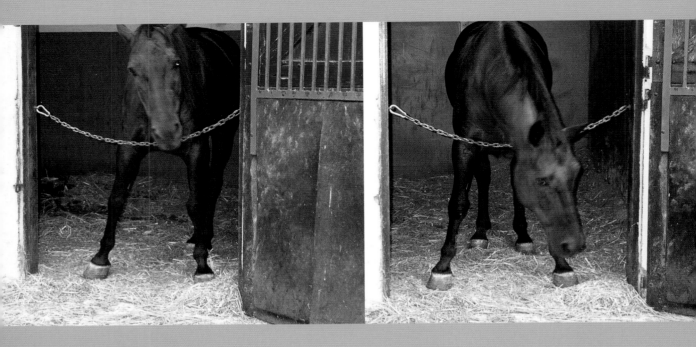

# Case Study: A Weaver

A crowd had gathered in the indoor school. Caro, a Spanish gelding, was performing *doma vaquera*, the upbeat, active dressage derived from Andalusian cattle herding. The horse's black coat was white with a foam of sweat and spittle as he laboured to perform flying lead changes. His head had been hauled down to his chest by a long-shanked curb bit; rowelled spurs were being pushed into his bleeding sides.

'…transferring all his weight from one leg to the other… he would swing from side to side oblivious to everything, hypnotized.'

Caro lived in the luxury stables with the other private liveries. His name was written above the door in tiles and rosettes were pinned along the beams. Caro spent most of his time doing the 'sway of the bear', as the Spanish call weaving. He had perfected the movement by leaning his chest on the chain across his doorway and swinging his head in a huge figure-of-eight, transferring all his weight from one leg to the other in the process. He would swing from side to side oblivious to everything, hypnotizing himself with the movement. The other liveries were similar – of Spanish blood, a breed renowned for their tolerance of difficult situations. Yet all were showing signs of stress. One lolled his tongue out of the side of his mouth, two bobbed their heads constantly, and a fourth turned away whenever anyone approached.

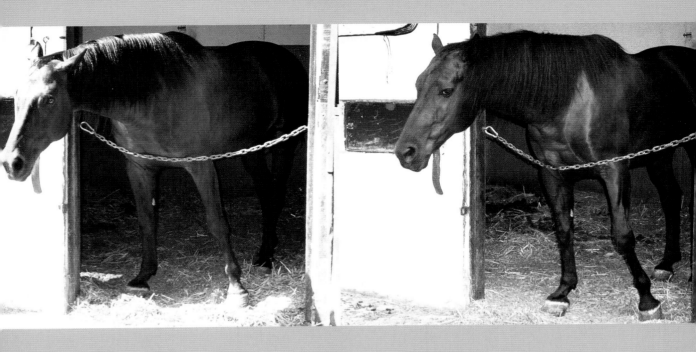

# Is it boredom or stress?

The livery owners were weekend cowboys who marched around in spurs and made their horses prance about to impress onlookers. They were not deliberately mistreating their horses but they were insensitive, and they could not understand why they were greeted by flattened ears. It wasn't just the spurs and the heavy hands that the horses hated, but the whole manner of the men: they were abrupt in both movement and voice. The animals' lives were made up of long periods isolated in enclosed boxes, interrupted by bursts of careless handling and pain. They never had the time and space to be sociable grazers;

food came in concentrated spurts. Monday was starvation day because the stable lad was off, so no hay was given.

Caro's owner attributed his horse's stress to the time that he had recently spent being schooled in *doma vaquera*. It was explained to the owner that the weaving was affecting Caro's brain chemistry, so the horse was likely to reach a point where it would be impossible to break the habit. Weaving would be the only thing he wanted to do. If the prospect of a junkie horse were not enough, the animal would also become useless by ruining his joints. As long as the horse found his work and competing stressful, the problem would continue. Using physical restraint to prevent the behaviour would

not solve the underlying psychological problem.

The owner realized he had to do something and took Caro away for a weekend's riding in the country. Whether he would change the animal's living conditions was another matter. Some people do not like to see their horses in a field and covered in mud.

## Conclusions

Caro's problems were caused by:

- Being kept in a loosebox all day, every day.
- No contact with other horses.
- Difficult, uncomfortable work and competing.

# Stressful Experiences: Weaning

There are a number of very stressful experiences we impose on horses that could be compared to human experiences such as moving house, divorce and bereavement.

The importance of consideration when weaning a foal cannot be overstated. In nature, weaning is not the total separation of the mare from her offspring, but the time at which a mare stops suckling her young. This is usually between nine months and a year, although it sometimes occurs later. Either shortly before or immediately after a new foal is born, the mother refuses to feed the previous year's foal and may be aggressive towards him for a short time. However, they are still together and maintain a relationship that will carry on for years.

Eventually, young horses form other bonds, especially with their siblings, and most leave the herd, although some stay with their mother's group. Family members even maintain friendships when living in other groups. I knew a mare that had lived with her daughters until they were adults. Years later, she used to recognize both of them by sight at shows.

What we humans call weaning is actually orphaning. The foal is suddenly removed from his mother, sometimes before he is six months old – the equivalent of separating a toddler from his parents. The foal is usually shut in a loosebox with the top door closed and the mare is taken away; the foal is then left to calm down. Sometimes a number of foals will be put together, all of them distraught at being apart from their mothers.

This is an extremely traumatic experience that may result in the foal crib-biting or weaving for the first time, thereby laying the foundations for establishment of these behaviours. Crib-biting may also be reinforced by the sudden introduction of a high-concentrate diet that results in stomach discomfort. Some behaviours, such as crib-biting or weaving, may unexpectedly surface at times of stress later in life and can be traced back to weaning, although we do not always have the information to make such associations.

The foal's social education is damaged at weaning, when he is placed in a group of other weanlings with no adults to teach acceptable behaviour. Naturally, a

■ **Stay away!**
With a scowl the mare is telling her yearling daughter to keep away from her new foal. Gradually the yearling was allowed to make contact with her sister and a firm friendship was formed.

foal would never live in a society that had no differentiation of age and sex, and a young horse learns about breeding and raising youngsters from the group. Some domesticated mares have never seen a foal until they give birth to one and they may reject their new offspring.

So how can we make separation more humane? First, we can leave the mare and foal together for as long as possible. Occasionally, a mare that is not in foal again may continue feeding her offspring for years. Provided that this does not affect the mare's condition adversely and/or make working the horses difficult, there is no harm in it. Separation can be introduced gradually and the two treated just as any other two horses. A mother will remain friends with her offspring, and a mare does not usually accept sexual advances from her colt foal. For example, the mother of my younger horse shows absolutely no interest in him when she meets him. She is much more pleased to see my other gelding, particularly when she is in season.

As with all horses, mare and foal will need to become accustomed to being separated and going out alone, because this will be part of their lives. As a youngster gets older he becomes more independent, but under natural conditions even at a year old a foal will spend nearly half his time within 20m (25yd) of his mother. Some foals virtually wean themselves, preferring the company of more interesting horses. Some mares have enough of being pushed around by their foals and make it clear they want to be left alone.

In some cases, weaning may be necessary: for example, if the mare is in poor condition she may benefit from not having to feed a youngster. However, a mare in good condition should not suffer from a few extra months of suckling. If the foal has to be sold eventually, then perhaps this could be delayed until he is a little older. Walking the foal out with the mare, allowing him to run free if possible, will increase his confidence and give him an oppor-

tunity to explore away from his mother.

Sometimes a mare will kick a rowdy foal and removing the foal may be necessary to prevent injury. If we know the mare and foal will have to be separated at a certain age, we can introduce separation gradually. Panicking foals can injure themselves, so care is needed. A possible sequence of events is as follows, although a great deal will depend on the individual horses and circumstances.

❍ Once the foal is becoming more independent, the mare can be taken away for short periods, as long as the foal has a friend with him. Begin by taking the mare to the other side of the paddock fence for a couple of minutes, where the foal can still see and be close to her, then return her to the field. Gradually increase the distance and time for which they separated.

❍ Mare and foal can then be separated physically, by putting them in neighbouring paddocks where they can see and touch each other. Both horses must have company.

❍ As the foal becomes accustomed to this arrangement, the mare can be taken out of sight for increasing periods of time.

The most important thing is to build up the time for which mare and foal are separated very gradually, with progress depending on the reaction of both horses. Distress and panic are to be avoided at all costs.

Ideally, the foal can stay with other members of the group into which he was born while his mother is taken away, as this will provide him with the security of familiar horses. If this is not possible, providing an older friend for the foal before weaning will reduce the upset when the final separation takes place, because the foal will be living with someone he knows and can rely upon. Placing a foal in a group of similarly distressed orphaned foals will *not* provide the confident company that he needs.

# Stressful Experiences: Loading and Unloading

I was once helping to load a stallion into a horsebox. He was reluctant to go in, but was gradually edging forward. He finally came halfway up the ramp after me, at which point the driver whacked him on the rump with a schooling whip. The horse promptly leapt sideways off the ramp and bolted.

This illustrates the problem with how we load horses. We neglect to reward the behaviour we want, and we begin fights that make the horse just want to get away from us. Most people have come across horses that do not load well, from those that refuse to move to those that begin to fight as soon as they see a vehicle. We need to remember that most horses need to be taught how to load: the basic idea of going into, and being shut in, a small space that then starts to move with you inside is not one that appeals to horses! A gradual process of feeding the horse near the vehicle, then on the ramp, then inside is one of the simplest ways to achieve this. Horses that trust their handler and are used to new experiences may walk straight into a trailer or wagon, even if they have never seen it before.

However, there is a significant number of horses that do not want to go anywhere near a vehicle, usually because they associate the process with trauma — either deliberate, such as being frightened into loading, or accidental, such as experiencing a bad journey. Every time a horse is forced into a horsebox the problem gets worse. If you have to fight a horse into

### ■ First time loading/1

A relaxed first approach to the wagon. It is not really advisable for the handler to sit down when loading a horse for the first time, but it demonstrates how relaxed the situation is.

The horse has time to sniff and examine, and to establish there is food ahead. Then a movement behind distracts him and he stops. Note the ear towards the camera. With attention forward, on the food, the horse then walked in (see overleaf).

■ **First time loading/2**
A common approach to loading, using brute force. How is this filly going to feel when she next sees a trailer? Will she be any easier to load? Note the reaction of the grey horse on the right.

loading or physically push and drag him in, the behaviour is not being addressed.

A horse that is difficult to load will need to be retrained. The alternative is to have a fight every time, with no guarantee that the horse will load at the end of it. The retraining process will involve gradually getting the horse first to approach the trailer or horse-box and then to step into it. This may have to take place step by step and inch by inch, with the aim of each training session being to get closer – not necessarily to go all the way in.

When teaching a horse to approach the vehicle, it is important to keep his attention in front. For this reason, it is better not to have anyone behind him. However, some horses can be persuaded to load by making it less comfortable for them to go away from the vehicle than towards it. Having someone behind the horse who waves their arms, a jacket or a plastic bag if the horse steps back may work. This is not the same as frightening the horse forward: it is simply making the desired behaviour – facing the vehicle and not backing away – more comfortable than the unwanted behaviour. As soon as the horse focuses in the direction we want, the waving stops and every positive move in the right direction is rewarded. A whip is best avoided because most horses associate it with being hit.

Similarly, unloading needs to be undertaken with time and care, giving the horse enough rope so that his head can move freely while maintaining control should he move suddenly. For a horse to reverse out of a trailer and down a ramp safely, he needs to be able to look behind. If unloading forwards, some horses jump down the ramp at first, so be prepared for this by giving him plenty of room and making sure that there is nothing in the way, including yourself.

> **The foundations for improving loading are:**
> 1 Do not load when you are in a hurry. When teaching loading, do it on a day when you do not have to go anywhere.
> 2 Do not use force or get into a fight.
> 3 Take regular breaks to allow both horse and handler to relax.
> 4 Make sure the vehicle is safe, and drive slowly and with care.
> 5 Take the horse for a ride in the vehicle and then back home.
> 6 If the horse enjoys exploring new places, take him somewhere new.

# Stressful Experiences: Travelling

Being moved in a horsebox or trailer is stressful and tiring for horses. A few hours' travelling is enough to trigger release into the blood of the chemicals associated with stress. Because most of us do not see our horses travelling, we do not know how they respond.

Some horses prefer to travel diagonally, facing backwards with their forelegs splayed for balance. However, most vehicles only allow one facing direction. Recent research suggests that horses will always try to see out of a vehicle, so large windows are of great benefit in reducing travelling stress.

Travelling can be difficult and uncomfortable for the horse, for a number of reasons:

○ The effort that a horse puts into maintaining his balance when the vehicle is changing speed and going around corners is considerable.
○ If the horse is facing forwards, he will be thrown backwards and forwards by acceleration and deceleration.
○ If the horse is facing sideways, he will be thrown backwards and forwards by any lateral movement of the horsebox.
○ If the horse leans on his rump to balance, this may cause damage to the dock over a long journey. Lucy Rees has a method of fitting wedges across the back corners of the compartment, so that the horse can rest his 'cheeks' against them without putting pressure on his dock.)
○ Tying the horse so that he cannot lean on his rump means he will have to adjust his balance continually, and the longer the journey the more stressful and tiring this will be.
○ If the horse is facing sideways, the camber of the road often means that he is actually

pointing slightly downhill, with extra weight on his forelegs.

Travelling stress may not be noticed because its effects may only become apparent some days later – for example, as colic. Horses sweat during travel and may not be relaxed enough to drink on the journey,

so dehydration and a slowing down of the digestive system may occur as a result. A horse that cannot lower his head during a long journey may suffer respiratory disorders.

So, how can we make travelling better?

○ Build and adapt vehicles so that horses can face in the direction they appear most comfortable.
○ Drive slowly and carefully, especially on winding roads and when manoeuvring around sharp bends and corners.

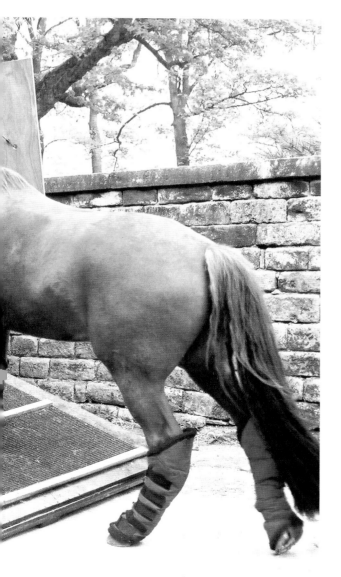

○ Make sure you accelerate and brake smoothly and gently. Use your gears to slow down, rather than your brakes.
○ Fit the box or trailer with windows so that the horse can see out. If this is not possible, at least allow the horse to see out of the back of a trailer by leaving the top doors open and tying the horse loosely enough so that he can turn his head (but not turn around). You will need to make a judgment as to whether your horse is likely to be frightened by the sight of vehicles drawing up behind or overtaking. Wagon windows facing outwards will be scraped by tree branches, and this can be very alarming.
○ Give adequate rest time, preferably by unloading the horse. A break every four hours is recommended, but on difficult journeys more regular breaks may be needed. After travelling, a horse may take an hour before he is relaxed enough to drink and urinate.
○ Do not tie up the horse too short. He needs to be able to change his body position.
○ Arrive with enough time to let the horse relax before having to compete.
○ Consider travelling time as part of the day's exercise. Some horses show signs of distress on the journey home because they are tired.
○ Do not overclothe the horse. Boots, bandages and rugs will exacerbate the stress if the horse is overheating. Ensure plenty of ventilation and consider whether a rug is really necessary.
○ Occasionally take the horse somewhere for a relaxed ride. This will avoid him associating travelling with stressful events such as competing.

■ **Calmly in**
The loading process took four minutes and the message to the horse was that this is no big deal.

# Stressful Experiences: Medical Attention

Some horses find medical attention upsetting and will spot a vet instantly. This is not unreasonable, as medical attention can be painful. However, a horse that has always been handled sympathetically and has been taught to accept handling will generally tolerate unpleasant attention.

There are several ways in which we can make the experience more tolerable for the horse:

○ It is essential that the people involved remain calm and relaxed.

○ As the horse becomes more upset by the treatment, breaks will help to allow the animal to calm down.

○ If a horse has problems with a particular type of treatment – for example, dentistry – it may help to accustom him to various elements of the process over time. If it is affordable, the dentist could come out the first time simply to fit the gag and not attempt further treatment until the horse accepts that process.

## Using Restraint

To save time and/or keep handlers safe, restraining methods are often used:

○ Twitching makes some horses freeze, enabling them to be treated. Some people claim that it does not hurt the horse but produces a release of painkilling chemicals into the brain. However, it seems logical that painkilling chemicals are released in response to extreme pain and I would avoid twitching if possible.

○ Sedation may help, providing the medication actually calms the horse mentally, rather than just disabling him physically. In the latter case, he will be frightened but unable to react. There are always risks associated with medication, and tranquillizers may have no effect on a horse that is already upset.

○ Physical or medical restraint will never tackle the cause of the behaviour or change the horse's attitude to medical attention.

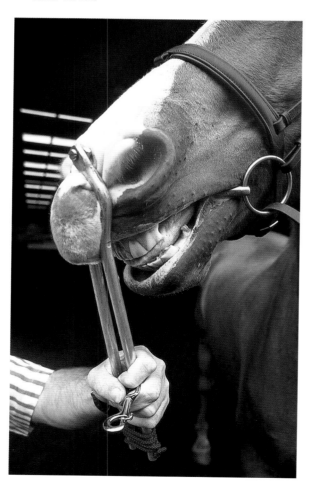

**■ Twitching**
The twitch – along with lip chains, Chifney bits and studded halters – uses pain and discomfort to inhibit the horse. Surely helping him to accept attention would be a better starting point?

# Stressful Experiences: Hoof Care

A horse's survival depends on his feet and legs. It is an amazing act of trust that horses allow us to nail pieces of metal on to their hooves. However, difficulties with shoeing can occur, including leaning on the farrier, refusing to lift a leg, pulling the foot away, and kicking and fighting. Most problems with shoeing arise from the horse never having been taught to have his feet handled or from trauma associated with being shod. The latter may be mistreatment, or pain caused accidentally – for example, by misplacement of a nail.

Teaching a horse to be shod begins with the foal, if possible. In the first few weeks of life, he can be taught to lift a leg and have his foot held, a lesson that will not be forgotten. Having his hooves handled, tapped and moved around becomes part of the youngster's daily life before shoeing. To prevent the horse leaning on people, just support the foot lightly while picking it out rather than acting as a prop.

The farrier's role is crucial in maintaining a horse that is happy to be shod, and it is courteous to prepare the horse properly so that the farrier is not at risk of being injured. When shoeing for the first time, let the horse see what is happening. A horse tied up on 45cm (18in) of rope cannot turn or lower his head; if the farrier then marches up to the horse, slaps him on the rump, picks up a hoof and begins to rive, rasp and hammer away, it would be sensible at least to allow the horse to see what is happening.

Holding the horse allows him to see what is taking place while still being under control, and to sniff (but not bite) the farrier if he wants to. Later, the horse can be tied on a loose rope or, if necessary, tied up short – for example, if he is trying to bite the farrier.

Another essential consideration is that the horse must be standing in a balanced way in order to be able to hold up his leg. Being out of balance is one reason for the horse's tendency to lean or try to pull the leg away. Horses often begin to get difficult because they are uncomfortable. The positions in which they must hold their legs for shoeing are unnatural, so it may be necessary to allow the horse to rest if he begins to fidget. This discomfort is exacerbated by tying too short, because the horse cannot move into a comfortable position.

Some horses spend their lives being twitched, sedated and, in one case I know, anaesthetized for shoeing. These are unacceptable actions if we are striving to improve our horses' lives. A horse that is difficult to shoe needs careful retraining. This involves taking time to break down the process into tiny stages, then build it back up again to shoeing. Each stage of the process must be positively reinforced by rewarding the horse (see pages 106–7). It may begin with just rewarding the horse for allowing his hoof to be touched, then requesting that the foot be raised, until eventually the horse accepts shoeing. Training sessions should be kept short and tempers calm.

# Stressful Experiences: Changing Homes

It is very unnatural for horses to move homes in the way that we humans consider normal. Naturally, friendship bonds and home areas are long lasting, often permanent, although when there is change horses do cope with it. We move horses from yard to yard with little thought; we take mares from their homes to new environments to be covered by stallions.

> **Changing places may entail:**
> 1 Loss of friends.
> 2 Loss of a familiar place.
> 3 Loss of familiar humans.
> 4 New routine.
> 5 New expectations.

When we acquire a horse, we are often warned that he will spend some time 'trying it on'. This is an unhelpful way of viewing what is happening. We must bear in mind that the horse will be having to

learn everything about us and the new place. Our expectations, the words we use, the aids we use and the routines we follow are all new to the horse. Former owners may never have ridden the horse out alone; they may have trained him to respond to particular words on the lunge.

These are the details that may preoccupy us as new owners, but the change of companions and place is of far more importance to the horse. Not only has he lost his friends, and perhaps his mother, he now has to enter an established herd and get to know the members, or alternatively adapt to being alone. If the horse is particularly stressed by the whole process, he is not going to respond in the ways he responded at his last home. Even a horse that appears to be testing all the rules for the sake of it will soon respond to clear 'answers' from the owner as to what is acceptable.

To alleviate the problems we can:

- ○ Find out as much as possible about the commands and aids the horse understands from the previous owner.
- ○ Give the horse a few weeks to settle in. Do not expect to compete on him as soon as he arrives.
- ○ Turn the horse out. If he can spend time grazing all day and has space, he will relax more quickly.
- ○ Give him a friendly companion if possible, or keep him separate from but close to other horses.
- ○ Spend time getting to know the horse and building a relationship with him (see Chapter 6).

---

■ **Apprehension**
This ex-racehorse is clearly concerned about being separated from her friends, but she is still relaxed, aided by the relaxation of her rider.

## Cruelty and Competition

The desire to win leads some people to inflict cruelty on horses. Such practices include:

○ Tying down the heads of lead-rein ponies and leaving them in the stable, in order to make them drop their head when the child takes hold of the reins.

○ Wrapping clingfilm (plasticwrap) around the necks of show hacks to produce muscle wastage to create the 'desirable' neck shape.

○ Putting ginger into the rectum of show Arabs to make them elevate their tails and look more showy.

○ Using electric shocks to punish showjumpers that refuse or knock down fences.

■ **Dislike**
A clear expression of dislike of jumping can be seen on this pony's face. Ears pinned flat, mouth tight and attention backwards: this expression never changed however much he was jumped (see pages 124–6).

■ **Enthusiasm**
Same rider, different reaction. This pony is happy with jumping, as demonstrated by his pricked ears and relaxed eye and mouth.

# Stressful Experiences: Introducing New Horses

The introduction of a new horse into a herd usually leads to friction. This is as true in natural-living horses as in domestic ones. However, the level of aggression among domestic horses tends to be higher. Competition for space, resources and companions means a newcomer may be subjected to hostility.

The method of introducing a new member depends on the dynamics of the group and the facilities available. A relaxed group with plenty of space and food will have lower levels of tension to begin with; horses that have been fully socialized will be safer, because they understand the rituals of meeting strangers. One or more of the ideas set out below can be adapted to the situation, which depends on the individual personalities of group members. Horses do not feel fully introduced to each other until they have been free to sniff and touch with no barriers. Horses that act aggressively across barriers are often much calmer when given full access to each other.

○ Remove hind shoes, and front shoes where possible. A warning kick from an unshod hoof does much less damage than one from a shod hoof.

○ Partition off part of the field with an electric fence, so that the newcomer is physically separated while the group becomes accustomed to his presence.

○ Introduce the newcomer to one of the herd members away from the rest of the group, so that they form a bond. This may be a non-aggressive horse, or could be a more aggressive horse that prefers some company to none – the psychological effect of isolation from the herd will make him much more amenable to the newcomer.

○ Introduce the newcomer to each of the herd members individually.

○ Allow horses to get to know each other over fences or stable partitions.

○ Ride the new horse out with members of the group individually.

○ Make sure there is plenty of space for disputes to be settled by the new horse running away rather than being cornered and perhaps attacked and injured.

# 6 The Horse-Human Relationship

*'The horse's ears now stopped swiveling and turned backward. He suddenly dropped his head. At last, finding my voice, I said, "Jerimiah! Don't buck me off! You're a good horse, and I'll take good care of you! Just walk, please." His head came up, and he walked forward.'*

The All-True Travels and Adventures of Lidie Newton, *Jane Smiley*

In considering our interactions with horses, we need to ask the question: 'What is the basis of the relationship going to be?'

A common answer to this question is that we have to be the boss and always win. The effect of this is that we have a tendency to bully horses. Why do we do this? In order to answer this question, we need to explore ideas about dominance in horse societies, because there is a lot of misunderstanding of the issue.

The 'boss' approach is based on a belief about horse society that we could call the myth of the dominant stallion. There is a lot of evidence to counter this myth. Long-term studies of feral and domestic horses living under natural conditions show that horse society is far more co-operative and friendly than is often thought. There has been a change in focus to considering the importance of a lead mare, but closer examination reveals that this, too, is a simplification.

# Dominance Hierarchies and *Alpha* Horses: Fact or Fiction?

■ **Curiosity**
This stallion is interested in getting to know humans and has chosen to do so, despite the distractions around him.

The horse is essentially a co-operative and social animal. So are humans, a lot of the time. The existence of dominance relationships in both species can be overstated: are all human interactions based on strict principles of dominance? If I want to arrange to go out with a friend, we negotiate the day, time and place. If I get dominant and say 'We are going to this restaurant and you have no say in the matter,' I won't have a friend for very long. Similarly, workplace bullies do not have mutually beneficial relationships with their staff.

Most of the time, the only power that horses exert over each other is to say 'Move away from me.' This may be a horse wanting another horse to move out of his personal space, or it may be a stallion driving a straying foal back to the group. Equine dominance is not a way of saying 'Go over there, trot in a circle, gather some grass for me, then come back here because I say so.'

In a domestic situation, horses are often forced to be in each other's body space. Looseboxes are sometimes woefully small and bare paddocks overcrowded. This means that instances of horses telling each other where to go are much more frequent than in wild horses. A bucket of food or the desire to be first through the gate provide sources of dispute that rarely exist in nature. A strict pecking order will emerge in situations of high competition.

A dominance hierarchy is one in which Animal A at the top bosses Animal B, who in turn bosses Animal C. It is not the natural arrangement of horse society, yet many people treat their horses as if it were and use it as the basis of their training. Researchers and observers of horses have tried a variety of techniques to identify hierarchies, only to find that none existed. The facts that emerge are as follows:

❍ In free-living horse societies with no human interference, it is not possible to work out a dominance hierarchy within a group.
❍ A horse that may appear dominant in one situation may not be in another.

■ **Co-operation**
Trainer Mark Rashid working in the round pen. The Arab is quite content to interact and may leave if he wants to. The gelding was being long-lined and lunged within a couple of sessions.

### ■ Competition

A classic scenario for the emergence of a dominance hierarchy. Having been ridden for six hours without water, members of this group are carefully organized in their approach to the trough. The black mare is the oldest and approaches first; the others are being careful to keep their distance but are working their way closer to the water.

The black mare is willing to share with her friend, the dun. The young bay mare warns the three-year-old gelding to wait his turn. However, even in such a pressured situation there is no actual violence, and the horses avoid each other to ensure all runs smoothly. If the result of dominance is avoidance, how can it possibly help us with training the horse?

○ When researchers have tried to identify a hierarchy, they have had to introduce unnatural competition in order to do so.

○ The most important factor in who gives way to whom is age. Youngsters generally defer to adults.

○ Horses use avoidance to prevent disputes – for example, bands of horses will wait in turn at watering holes and some horses will avoid others.

If we try to apply the dominance hierarchy principle as a basis for training horses, we find that it doesn't work. The rationale for the existence of dominance hierarchies is that they enable the horse to avoid aggression and injury: the subordinate animal reads the signs from the dominant animal and moves away, so no one gets hurt.

However, in training animals by the 'show him who's boss' method, we destroy this dynamic. We act aggressively and exert dominance *while keeping the animal with us*. The horse, whose first action is to move away from aggression and who understands that this is what is required of him by the situation, is actually being punished while at the same time being deprived of the ability to carry out the correct course of action.

So, a trainer who believes that dominance is the way to approach horses actually abuses the principle by destroying the basis on which it works — that is, allowing movement away from aggression. Beating a horse while sitting on his back makes no sense to the horse: the animal is frightened and understands that the rider is saying 'Go away from me,' but he is not being allowed to follow the instruction. Equally, when working a horse loose in a round pen (see page 116) the animal is free to move but not to leave the situation completely, so round-penning can be just as domineering as 'traditional' methods if the trainer chooses to use it in this way.

# *Alpha* Horses and Aggression

Trainers talk about *alpha* animals, usually identified as horses that aggressively boss and bully other horses, and sometimes us. Some trainers apply the term *alpha* to horses that lead. Thus the meaning of the term *alpha* itself has become confused.

*Alpha* is actually a scientific term applied in studies of hierarchies. Each animal in the hierarchy is assigned a Greek letter from *alpha* through to *omega*, with *alpha* as the most dominant. In wolves, for example, *alpha* has traditionally been assigned to the breeding pair. This has given rise to the idea that humans have to be the top of the pack when interacting with animals. However, even scientists who study wolves are questioning the existence of dominance hierarchies in the canine world, pointing out that wolf packs are family groups and the breeding pair the parents. Dog trainers are also asking whether dominance is the correct basis for their training methods.

The assignment of *alpha* status to horses is a misuse of the term and has little meaning when we are looking at our relationships with horses. The reality is that *alpha* is being assigned to horses that are aggressive or that simply do not understand boundaries, yet aggression does not necessarily imply dominance. A horse that is pulling faces and threatening other horses all the time is not necessarily gaining any advantage by doing so.

As we have seen, the incidence of aggression in free-ranging horses is extremely low. Among feral mares that have not been forced into competitive situations by humans there is very little aggression, and the nature of that aggression is less serious — threats are more common than actual violence. So perhaps the bullying, aggressive, so-called *alpha* horse is actually the one who is most pressured by the system in which he is being kept, or who does not understand what is being asked of him, or who simply does not like what he is being made to do.

A horse that is highly aggressive to others may be giving signs that he is under pressure due to his living conditions and it is our responsibility to address this. Equally, if there are high levels of aggression the horse at the bottom of the pile may become nervous or depressed. Some horses have learned to be aggressive towards others and this behaviour may continue even when living conditions improve, although a decrease in hostility will usually be seen with time.

The expectation of seeing 'pecking orders' leads us to notice aggressive actions. We do *not* spot the more subtle interactions that serve to build relationships. These 'friendly' interactions are known as affiliative behaviours and may involve such actions as gentle approaches or being close to another horse when grazing. The person who only sees the horses when they are crowded at the gate in winter waiting for food will see aggression. If they spent time watching the horses together at grass in summer, a very different form of communication would be observed. Interestingly, aggressive gestures are often ignored by the horse they are aimed at, so what does this tell us about hierarchies?

## Submission?

To assert that relationships are based on dominance it has to be demonstrated that the dominated party shows submission. Submission based on dominance hierarchies is a way of saying 'I accept I am lower in status than you, don't hurt me.' Flattening the ears and lunging are a signal to another horse to move away that is often interpreted as domination. So is the other horse showing submission by moving away?

A comparison between horses and dogs is useful here. Dogs have a large repertoire of gestures, traditionally called submissive, designed actively to communicate they are not a threat to another dog (or human). They cringe, flatten their ears, show their gums, lie down and roll over. Although our understanding of horse body language is poor, it is apparent that adult horses display no equivalent grovelling actions. They simply move away, perhaps flattening the tail and dropping the rump to avoid getting bitten. If they cannot get away, the action of dropping the rump may be develop into 'bouncing' the back end at the threatening horse, finally followed by a defensive kick.

Foals mouth ('snap' or 'champ') to divert aggression (see page 24). The signal given by mouthing seems to be 'I am not a threat to you, I'll get out of your way if you insist, but I prefer to stay and talk to you' – which is not necessarily the same as saying 'I am subordinate to you.' A mare being forced to accept mating may freeze in fear and exhaustion, but again this is not a signal to say, 'OK, you're more dominant than I am, I'll do what you want.' If it were,

■ **Affiliative behaviour**
These are actions that create bonds between individuals. Despite having lived together for six years, these two geldings make regular contact during the day.

## Foal Communication

Why should it be that foals show a submissive gesture? A young horse has to explore everything and everybody. He has to introduce himself to his companions and learn about social relations from them. Therefore, he actively seeks out other horses while still learning the signs and gestures he needs. In addition, a new foal is a source of curiosity in a group of horses so they want to interact with him, while he lacks the mental and physical know-how to move away should the situation require it. The mouthing is probably a buffer designed to help a foal out of social situations that an older, wiser horse does not get into.

mares would always passively accept mating from domineering stallions, which they certainly do not.

So, when trainers talk about horses showing submissive gestures such as licking and chewing or dropping the head, there is no evidence that this is the case. What we are probably seeing is something that we, the humans, interpret as a horse giving up or relaxing. It is likely that the horse is not actively trying to communicate anything to us. The head dropping could be a result of fatigue in the back muscles from trotting around with the head raised in alarm. The licking and chewing may be a displacement activity to divert the horse from the conflict he is feeling between the desire to stop running and the fear of the situation, or it may be relaxation as he realizes that no harm is coming to him. It is not a horse saying to the human 'Don't hurt me, I want to be your friend.' If we gave the horse the option, he would simply do what he would do if another horse were pressuring him – that is, go away.

# The Alternative to Domination

So what is the basis of our relationship with the horse to be? With what do we replace 'show him who's boss'?

Animal behaviourists use the term 'affiliative behaviours' to describe actions that promote cohesion and bonds between animals. Horses show a range of such behaviours, including mutual grooming, approaching and touching. The motivation behind these behaviours is the maintenance of social relationships, arising from the horse's desire to be with others. If we focus on the affiliative behaviour of horses and the way they co-operate, synchronize, lead and follow, instead of trying to dominate them, we have a basis for training that they already understand.

When properly socialized as young animals, horses also learn the limits of acceptable behviour – for example, that they must not kick other horses. This means that if we are clear and reasonable in communicating what behaviour is acceptable, we do

■ **Affiliative behaviour**
Mutual grooming is pleasurable to horses and seems to cement bonds of friendship.

not need to allow horses to walk all over us in the belief that we are being nice to them. A relationship based on trust, clear direction, consistent treatment and defined boundaries works with horses. It makes them comfortable because they know what is expected of them, what they can expect of us and that our judgment can be trusted not to put them in difficult situations.

We do not need to be rigid in our approach: flexibility comes when we understand that certain things are too difficult or stressful for this particular horse at this particular time. In order to do this, we must allow horses to express their feelings and, crucially, we need to learn to recognize when they are uncomfortable, distressed or simply struggling with an activity, and act on this knowledge.

### ■ Synchronization

A group of horses operates as one entity. The horses have fanned out while grazing, thereby giving the group an all-round view of the surroundings. This would be an advantage if there were predators around. Their positioning means that should they need to run, they would move in the same direction and quickly bunch together.

# Leadership and Followership

Many horse trainers today talk about leadership and the trainer putting themselves in the position of being a leader. But leading depends on someone following, and the dynamic of followership is perhaps more important.

Three horses – a hunter, a pony and a cob – are at pasture. The hunter is thirsty. She decides to head off to the stream to drink. The pony notices her going and sets off after her. The cob spots the other two and follows them.

What factor is at work in this case: dominance, leadership or followership? The hunter is not dominating the other horses. She does not demand that they all move to water. She could be described as leading, but her moving off to drink is not a social behaviour. She is motivated by her thirst, not by a conscious decision to influence the actions of the other horses. However, the pony is motivated by social behaviour. His following is a decision based on seeing the hunter move off. In fact, it is the

### ■ Following

This young horse is more than happy to follow a person for no reason other than that she seems to be going somewhere and he is curious. Note the older horse coming along as well.

pony's conscious action that affects the whole group's movement to water. Therefore, the driving force for the group behaviour that results in cohesion and cements the band as a social entity is the pony's followership.

The following day the pony is thirsty. He begins to move to water, then stops. He is aware that he is going out on his own. The cob finally notices that the pony has moved off and begins to follow. The cob passes the pony, who is waiting uncertainly. Once the cob is in the lead, the pony and the hunter follow. The whole group movement has again been held together by followership.

The following day the pony hears a loud noise and takes off running. The hunter and cob immediately follow, then stop and turn to assess the danger. Again, the following is the key action in the whole group's movement.

The point here is that the horses were prepared to follow any one of the group who set off with conviction. Horses hate uncertainty. Generally, they will go along with anyone, horse or human, who acts with conviction – but a vacuum of conviction has to be filled, so wavering will put a horse on guard. A rider communicating uncertainty about going over a jump will find that the horse makes a decision about the best course of action, which may be stopping, rushing over the fence or heading for the gate. Scientific studies show that the lead horse changes in different situations, although older horses tend to lead. The changing leader is borne out in observations of domestic horses: the horse that leads the herd to shelter is not always the one that leads the group back out to graze.

Allowing for a brief diversion into anthropomorphism (attributing human characteristics to animals, see page 23), let's consider a conversation between a horse and rider about a plastic bag caught on a fence. For the purposes of understanding, the conversation has been translated from body language into English.

**The rider's aim here is to get past the bag with the minimum of fuss:**

**Horse** [Stops and freezes] Oh my god – look at that! What is it?

**Rider** [Looks at plastic bag and remains relaxed, allowing the horse to stand] Let's see. Well, it's just a bag. Look carefully – it really won't hurt us.

**Horse** [Bobs head] I'm sure it must be dangerous.

**Rider** [Remains calm] Relax, it's nothing. I'm not bothered, why should you be?

**Horse** Well OK… but I think I'd prefer to give it a wide berth to keep my eye on it.

**Rider** [Asks horse to walk on] OK, let's go past gently, you keep looking. You can stop if you want to.

**Horse** [Tries to turn and run] I can't do it. I'm going home.

**Rider** [Turns horse back to face bag] No way. We're going past it, not turning round. [Gently but firmly keeps horse facing forward and asks horse to move on] Have another look at it. Don't turn round.

**Horse** [Head up in alarm] I can't walk past that.

**Rider** [Dismounts and leads the way] All right, I'll get off and go first. If it doesn't jump out at me, it won't at you.

**Horse** [Starts to follow rider past bag] OK, here we go! Phew. You were right.

Traditionally, we have been told that if we get off a horse to lead him past something, we have 'given in' to him. The belief is that the horse will learn to stop at objects and will do so in order to make us get off. From this viewpoint, the rider should have forced the horse past the bag, hitting him if necessary, so that control arises because the horse is more afraid of the rider than anything else. The relationship that develops is then based on physical restraint – and at some point the horse's fear of an external factor is going to outweigh his fear of the rider. We

**■ Trust**
This Exmoor weanling has experienced three weeks of human handling, having lived wild. He has learned that people are safe and he is happy to follow the handler on to the plastic sheet without being on a lead rope.

can guess that if horse and rider part company, the horse won't hang around waiting for the rider to get back on.

However, we can see that what we have actually done in the dialogue is to provide the horse with the opportunity to follow our more confident lead. The rider's aim of getting past the plastic bag with the minimum of fuss has been achieved. Because no lions jumped out, next time the horse will probably go forward with the rider on board, though he will still need to take his time. The key point is that the rider has demonstrated to the horse that they can be trusted to judge the safety of the situation. The rider said it was safe and it was. The rider also drew a firm line about what was acceptable. The horse was not allowed to turn and run.

This is a big building block in the process of the horse gaining confidence in the rider and will be carried into other situations, where the horse will trust the rider more readily. Besides, if horses really didn't

want us on their backs that much, they wouldn't let us get on in the first place.

A word of warning about the above scenario. If we swap roles with the horse and start saying 'Oh my god,' most horses, particularly green ones, won't take the reassuring role. By anticipating problems, tensing up and grabbing the reins, we are actually notifying our horses that there is something dangerous ahead. The herd works in this way: if one spots danger, the others will follow the line of attention. It is important to learn to control our reactions, through breathing and relaxation, so that we do not actually make a horse worry about a situation that he was not worried about to begin with.

The reward for this type of relationship can be seen in the following interaction I had with a horse:

| | |
|---|---|
| **Me** | [Freezing and grabbing the reins] Oh my god, I've brought us into a bog. |
| **Horse** | [Standing and looking] Yes, you have. |
| **Me** | [Relaxing and loosening the reins] I can't see any way out, can you get me out of here? |
| **Horse** | [Sniffing the ground] Well, let's see. It's this way, and over here… |

# Lessons From Feral Horses

Although aggression and dominance are less common in natural horse societies, they do occur in certain situations. By understanding that these behaviours are not the basis of feral horse groups but are linked to particular circumstances, we can work to reduce these behaviours in our own horses by adjusting their living conditions and the way we handle them.

Generally, a young horse will give way to an adult horse. Put another way, the grown-ups teach the children what is what, which is not surprising and also accounts for the observation that older mares usually lead the way.

## Mares

Mares are aggressive to their yearlings for a couple of days when their new foal is born, although this may be just a mild threat if the yearling approaches too closely. They will also show aggression to youngsters that are taking liberties – for example, someone else's foal trying to suckle, or a yearling getting too close.

In feral horses, the bigger the group of horses the more aggression appears in mares, and the situation that sparks most aggression is the introduction of a new mare. Keeping horses in large numbers relative to the space available and constantly introducing and removing members are common practices in our husbandry systems, so perhaps we need to think more carefully about our group set-ups.

## Stallions

An obvious display of aggression occurs in stallions competing for mares, yet it has been shown that

### ■ Cohesion

Horses constantly make contact with each other, even when they have been nearby. This young stallion touches his mares at intervals throughout the day. This mare is in foal to him, yet he is still interested in her even though she is not in season. The foal grazing with (and obscured by) the mare in the background is his daughter. The stallion interacted with all his offspring and was particularly friendly with one of his colt foals.

**■ Mutual benefit**
Horses allow birds to perch on their backs to remove parasites. This inter-species co-operation will be extended to humans if they find us pleasant to be with.

feral stallions spend up to 98 per cent of their time in non-aggressive activities. Real fighting is rare and disputes are usually resolved by stallions moving their respective groups apart or by posture threats. This is in keeping with how nature works to minimize injury. Wild horse studies show that stallions will often go through the posturing at a distance, then return to their bands with no obvious winner or loser. What a stallion does *not* usually do is chase off to find another stallion and give him a beating in order to 'show him who's running the show.' However, when a stallion is seriously angry, the stage of ritual posturing may be missed out and he will go straight for the fight.

Feral horse studies have shown that sometimes stallions will engage in forced mating (in human terms, rape), having chased the mare to the point of exhaustion. This is by no means the norm, however, and certainly occurs far less than in domestic matings, where forced mating is commonplace.

## Inter-Group Aggression

When resources are unusually limited, there may be aggression between horses — for example, when a water source freezes to a trickle. Generally, however, groups keep their distances and wait their turn, thereby avoiding inter-group aggression. This is shown on a larger scale by the fact that as horse numbers increase, horses search out greater ranges so that direct competition does not arise.

## Inter-Species Aggression

Feral horses will occasionally show aggression to other species such as deer or antelope if they are in immediate competition for resources. Occasionally, stallions and mares will drive off predators that are threatening their young. This inter-species aggression is seen when horses are kept with other herbivores and may also be directed towards dogs.

# Case Study: Crossing Water

I once got stranded trying to lead a three-year-old horse through a large, muddy puddle that completely covered the bridleway. He refused to move. A cyclist came along and kindly pushed from behind, but, like a cartoon donkey, the animal folded up like a concertina but would not budge. Using force and getting angry only made him panicky and less willing to step forward.

The cyclist headed home with instructions to phone my mum to bring me a coat and sandwiches. He had a half hour's ride ahead and was doubtful that I would still be there when he got home. 'I think I will,' I told him grimly. I was determined to sit there all night if necessary. An hour and a half later the youngster finally went through the water. I trotted him to the end of the track, turned him around so that we were facing home, and took him back through the puddle.

## Brain not brawn

This interaction demonstrates various dynamics:

○ My attempt to dominate (bully) the horse into crossing the water failed, but although a greater degree of force may have got him across, my aim was not to show him who was boss. Humans have the ability to think in ways horses cannot, which means that sheer brute force is not necessary.

○ My philosophy was that it was reasonable to ask him to go through water, because he was going to have to do it on a daily basis. Therefore, sitting there for an hour and a half until he crossed meant that (a) I had achieved my aim and (b) I had not reinforced his belief that water was to be avoided.

○ My advantage was a grim determination that I could outlast him. He had no alternative but to follow me through eventually because I did not let him turn round, go backwards or get comfortable and eat.

○ With hindsight, I could have anticipated the problem and taken steps to mitigate it – for example, by first approaching the puddle as we were homeward bound, earlier in the day and with some carrots in my pocket. However, horses are individuals and we do not always know how they are going to react.

■ **Is it safe?**
Training exercises in a safe environment allow the horse to indulge his natural caution and will prevent problems developing later.

# Exercises: On Dominance and Submission, Leadership and Followership

**1** Read the passage below about packhorse teams. The Galloway horses, or 'gals', were always loose and travelled in a string. Think of how the behaviour of the bell-horse (the horse that led the team) could be interpreted in terms of dominance, leadership or followership.

*'After starting the horses would generally be allowed to eat grass by the roadside or open spaces, as they went along; but the drivers when they considered they had had sufficient, would put on muzzles... If the bell-horse, while grazing, happened to get behind the others, as soon as it was muzzled it knew the real travelling for the day had commenced, and would bore and push until its own honoured place as leader was gained.... Occasionally the men would walk ahead a mile or so, in order to have a pint or a pipe at some well-known pub. The 'gals' understood this proceeding, and (if they were muzzled) would jog along as if their drivers were by their sides.*

*Pack Horse in the North*, S. Emily Lumb (1890)

## Ask yourself

☐ Is the bell horse dominating the other horses and ordering them where to go?
☐ Or does he head off in the direction he wants to and the others follow?
☐ Is the bell horse dominating the other horses and ordering them where to go?
☐ And where does the idea of dominance come into the action of the horses continuing their journey while the men rest in the pub? Nobody, horse or human, is forcing them to continue. They simply follow the horse in front.

**2** A pony wanders towards a cob, who responds by putting his ears back and thrusting his head at the pony, who stops and then moves away.

## Ask yourself

☐ Is the cob being aggressive? He could be said to be showing aggression to the pony or, if we think about personal space, he could be said to be defending his body space. If we accept the latter, we can interpret his actions as defensive rather than aggressive.

**3** A horse is in a field that has very little grass in it. There is a fence between that field and the one next door, where there is grass. The horse puts his head under the fence and stretches as far as he can to eat the grass in the neighbouring field. As he leans, he pushes the rail free of the fence post and so leans even further, thereby reaching more grass. He moves along the fence, puts his head under, and pushes. This time the rail does not come free, so the horse gives up and moves on.

## Ask yourself

☐ Is this horse 'exerting dominance' over the fence? Would we say the horse was 'trying it on' with the fence?
☐ If, instead of a fence, someone is holding the horse and he keeps pulling towards a patch of grass, is the horse trying to dominate the handler or simply trying to move to the grass?
☐ If the horse tries to tow one person, and succeeds because the person moves, is he being dominant or just treating the person in the way he treated the fence?
☐ And is he not being dominant if he tries to tow another person, but doesn't succeed?

The answer must be that on both occasions the horse is not thinking in terms of winning or losing for the sake of it – all he is trying to do is get to the grass.

# 7 Education and Training

*'There is no such whetstone... to encourage a will to learning, as is praise'*   The Schoolmaster, *Roger Ascham*

The aim of teaching and training our horses is to equip them to cope with us and with what we want them to do. This is a different approach to the usual idea of making horses submit to our will. Of course, we have to get the horse to do what we want, otherwise he would usually choose to spend all day in the field, but getting a horse to do what we want has to be done with sensitivity to the horse's experience of what we ask him to do. Degrees of brutality can make a horse do many things, but such an approach will result in a broken-spirited horse that acts like a robot, a horse that performs out of fear or, in some cases, a horse that meets violence with violence. We must always ask ourselves how well the horse copes with our choice of activity and our method of training.

# How Horses Learn

Coping with humans permeates the entire life of the horse, not just the time for which we are actually riding or driving him. For example, a stabled horse has to cope with the fact that he cannot make choices about how to spend his time; a horse that has a rider who is constantly giving aids while not requiring anything of the horse has to accommodate this. Some horses are amazingly good at picking out what is required despite all the buzzing confusion and inconsistency they experience from us.

So how do we make ourselves easier to cope with and, ideally, become creatures with which horses actually want to engage? Having made the horse's lifestyle as natural as possible to ensure a healthy mental state, we must then endeavour to understand how the horse learns.

We need to distinguish psychological learning from physical learning. For example, when learning to play basketball you have to be able to bounce the ball with either hand. I was motivated by my desire to play basketball and once I mentally understood that I would need to use my left hand as much as my right, I then had to train my body to dribble first with the right hand and then with the left. This body training is called motor learning and involves practising the action until the body is 'programmed' to do something that does not come naturally. Once I could dribble with my right hand, I then had to learn when to dribble with the left, and recognize the cues

that would make it a successful course of action. A horse experiences the same elements in learning.

There are many books outlining theories of learning in varying detail. In order to minimize confusion and technical language, I offer 11 points about how a horse learns:

## 1 Cues

For a horse to begin to associate a cue with an action, the cue must be given prior to the action beginning. To teach the word 'walk', begin to walk, then say the word just as the horse is preparing to walk. The word 'walk' will soon become the cue for the horse to begin the action.

## 2 Towards rewards

For a horse to associate a pleasant outcome (a positive reinforcer) with his action, the reinforcer must be given immediately the horse has completed the action. This may involve breaking down the action into steps. So, on the command 'back' the first weight-shift backwards is rewarded. As understanding increases, the horse has to do more – for example, take a whole step backwards. As learning progresses, this time-lag between the action and the reward can increase.

## 3 Towards comfort

When a horse gives the desired response in order to remove an unpleasant stimulus, this is called negative reinforcement. The unpleasant stimulus does not have to be harsh. For example, a gentle, repetitive tug and release on the headcollar to request that a horse turns his head towards the trainer may be enough to get the desired response. The horse will learn quickly, as long as his action really does remove the annoyance. If the tugging continues

---

**In order to learn the horse has to:**

1 Be motivated.

2 Understand what he has to do.

3 Be physically able to perform the task.

4 Learn to recognize the cues (aids) that we give him.

---

after the horse has turned his head, he will not realize that he has made the correct response and will become confused.

However, negative reinforcement is sometimes used in a way that upsets the horse – for example, when a trainer on the ground requests that the horse backs up by vigorously swinging the lead rope from side to side. The horse learns that if he does not back up when asked to do so the experience becomes increasingly uncomfortable (the trainer increases the swing of the rope), but he can bring an end to the discomfort by backing up.

## 4 Punishment or abuse?

Punishment is an unpleasant outcome of the horse's action that decreases the chance of the behaviour occurring again in the future. This means that if you are continually attempting to punish the horse for the same behaviour, the punishment is not working. So, if you have been whipping the horse for refusing fences for five years, yet it continues to refuse, technically you are not punishing it, but abusing it. You may well be making the problem worse.

For an action to be termed 'punishment', it would have to be clear that the horse had changed his behaviour as a result of this outcome. For example, if your horse routinely lunges at you to bite and you decide to deal with the behaviour by slapping his muzzle as it comes towards you, the slap is only punishment if after using it on a few occasions the horse stops lunging to bite.

So, we can see that to say the punishment for X is Y does not help us in training, because it will depend on whether the chance of the behaviour occurring again actually decreases, and this will depend on each individual case.

Our ideas about punishment are tied up with justice, revenge and retribution. Retributive punishment has no meaning to horses. With humans, punishment can take place after an event, because we understand

■ **Learning about humans**
It took six weeks for anyone to touch this foal owing to a protective mother, but once he discovered how nice humans could be he welcomed the attention.

that punishment can be separated from the action by time. Punishment exists for misbehaviour, and we understand that we can be punished even for something that happened years before. Sometimes we are actually relieved to be punished, as it helps us to deal with guilt. Horses do not think like this. Punishing a horse for giving the wrong response to a cue is counterproductive. A horse that is trained by indiscriminate punishment will be afraid of his trainer. He will never know what the correct response is if he is only ever punished for the wrong one.

## 5 Adaptation

A horse will get used to a particular stimulus and begin to ignore it – that is, he will adapt to the stimulus. This is vital in training because the horse becomes accustomed to all the strange things it encounters – for example, it stops running away every time it sees an umbrella. Conversely, if we misuse our cues the behaviour we desire may cease, because the horse will begin to ignore us. For example, the habit of continually applying pressure with the leg, even when the horse is doing what is required, will eventually lead to him ignoring the leg.

## 6 Association

Horses can both discriminate and generalize. If you visit your horse in the field regularly but only carry a headcollar when you are planning to ride, your horse will very quickly associate the headcollar with being ridden. A horse that has been mistreated by a man may generalize his dislike to all men, yet discriminate and allow women to handle him. Alternatively, he may discriminate between big men and small men, or he may generalize his fear of men to all humans. This gives us the option of trying different approaches to solving problems, in the belief that there must be something that works. It seems that the worse the experience, the more widely the horse will generalize – just to be sure he doesn't go through the same trauma again.

## 7 Shaping

Ignore the wrong response, reward the right one. A response to a cue that is ignored will often vanish, or technically 'extinguish', with time. One way that horses learn is by trial and error. Once they are tuned in to receiving a reward for the correct response, they will be more likely to make that response. Behaviour can be shaped by reinforcing each step towards the desired response.

## 8 Confusion

Be consistent in the cues you give. We confuse horses by changing the words and cues we use. Be aware that someone else may have used different cues and the horse may simply not understand what you are asking.

## 9 Awareness

Horses will learn things that we do not intend to teach them. If a horse is behaving in a certain way, it may be that you are inadvertently giving him signals to which you don't want him to respond. Tensing up (the cue) because you think the horse is going to be frightened is one example of providing an unintended cue. The horse will actually learn that there is something dangerous ahead and respond accordingly.

## 10 Responsiveness

Begin with a cue that you judge the horse will detect. The cues you choose will depend on what the horse knows, whether you want to use your voice, how you want to use your body and what you are aiming for. For example, imagine that you want the cue to walk on to be the lightest possible touch with your calves on the horse's sides. To teach this, you could first squeeze with your legs. If that does not get a response, you can increase the strength of the cue or introduce another one – for example, as you squeeze with you legs, you can also slap your thigh. Once the correct response is achieved, you can gradually reduce the strength of the cue. Riders often use spurs or whips habitually, without considering whether the horse can actually learn to respond to much lighter cues.

## 11 Variety

Horses learn quickly and remember well. Due to these abilities, it is better only to repeat an exercise to the point at which learning has been satisfactorily acquired. It is boring for a horse to have to keep repeating an exercise day after day just for the sake of it. A break between training sessions actually increases the rate of learning, because it allows the horse time to assimilate the learning experience and will often produce a much better response when the horse is brought back into the training situation. This means that we can introduce a variety of activities in training without harming the one on which we want to focus. We do not just have to school: we can trail ride too (and vice versa), as the activities actually complement each other. If a learned behaviour appears to be getting lost, then retraining may be introduced to maintain the behaviour.

## ■ The teaching process: opening a gate

This requires a sophisticated level of manoeuvring on the part of horse and rider, yet a young or novice horse will learn quickly because the exercise has a point. Breaking down the task into stages and working with clear cues, whether voice commands or aids; using rewards for correct behaviour; ignoring the wrong response; and simply re-presenting the task if it goes wrong will teach any activity effectively.

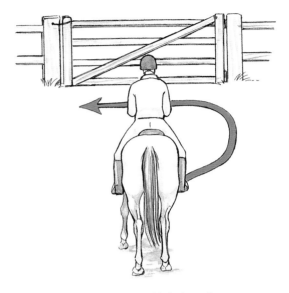

**I Ask the horse to walk a half circle and come parallel to the gate**
**Successful:** Reward and go to 2 (top right).
**Unsuccessful:** Turn away and re-present.

**2 Cue the horse to halt when you are level with the gate catch**
**Successful:** Reward and go to 3.
**Unsuccessful:** Re-present horse and try again.

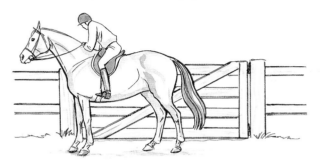

**3 Open the catch while the horse stands still**
**Successful:** Reward and go to 4.
**Unsuccessful:** If the horse has moved forward, cue him to back up until you are level with the gate catch again; if the horse has moved away, go back to 1.

**4 Cue the horse to turn on his forehand away from the gate as you open it**
**Successful:** Reward each step in the right direction.
**Unsuccessful:** Let go of the gate and re-present.

**5 Ask the horse to stand and wait with the gate open**
**Successful:** You are now ready to reverse the process to pass through the gate and close it.
**Unsuccessful:** Go back to the last successful stage and re-present from there.

# Fear

Fear will teach a horse very quickly, but he will not be learning what we want to teach him. Learning from frightening experiences is a survival mechanism to make animals avoid dangerous situations. A horse that has been frightened will have a strong memory of what frightened him, and this leads to him learning that this person/situation/activity is to be avoided at all costs.

If the horse has had a bad experience in a trailer, for example, it may be quite difficult to eradicate the negative feelings associated with that memory. Fear increases avoidance and indecision, and makes the horse afraid to try anything, thereby reducing his capacity to learn in the long term.

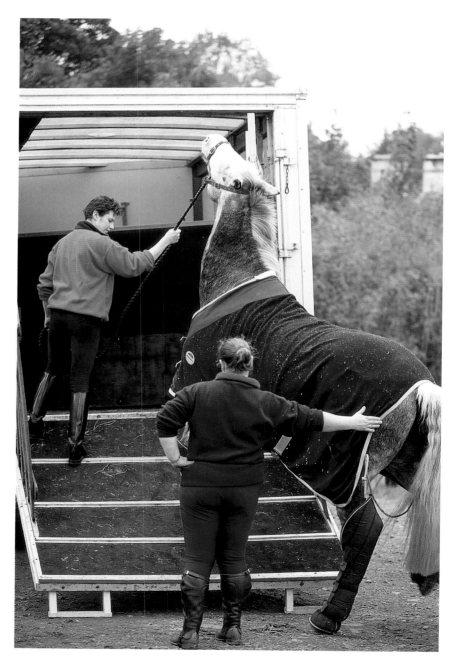

## Unintended Learning

You are riding a horse that startles at everything. What do you do when the horse spooks? Do you grab at the reins? Do you start talking softly, having been silent before? Do you tense up, expecting something bad to happen? Do you shout at the horse? Do you hit or kick him? If your behaviour occurs each time the horse is frightened, he will associate your actions with his fear. How about relaxing completely and totally ignoring the behaviour? What signal does this give to the horse?

■ **Reluctance to load**
A horse that associates loading with negative feelings will need to be retrained in a calm situation with no pressure of time.

# Rewards

It is striking how poor we are at telling horses when they have done the right thing, yet how quickly we tell them they have done something wrong. We also reward at the wrong time: for example, patting the horse as he is leaving the show ring. Once a horse is trained to expect rewards (positive reinforcement) he will begin to work towards them, which makes training easier and more enjoyable.

## Relaxation

Allowing relaxation mirrors natural situations. If there is a scare, horses will startle and maybe run; they will then relax once it is all over. It is therefore abusive if, having fallen off a horse that is then quietly grazing nearby, you pick yourself up, march up to the horse, grab the reins and yell at him. To the horse, the excitement has passed and he is being abused for grazing quietly.

Being allowed to stop an activity and relax is a reward that it is easy for the horse to understand. Releasing the rein when the horse has performed a desired action – for example, the first time that he collects for a step or two – is a clear reward that the horse will seek the next time, by trying the same behaviour – that is, collecting. The next time the horse may be asked to collect for five steps and is then rewarded. In this way, the desirable behaviour can be built up.

### ■ Which reward?

A horse being worked hard while schooling like this will appreciate the chance to stretch his neck and will understand that release on to a loose rein, held at the buckle, is an instant reward for his exertion.

**■ Petting**
Scratching the withers is an excellent way of rewarding a horse, and one that he understands naturally and that can be used when mounted. This youngster has not yet been started for riding, and provided he is treated well there should be no problems building on the relationship he has with people.

## Food

Using food rewards has to be clearly separated from giving titbits. Horses do not give each other food, so it is not a natural way of interacting. However, it is a very strong motivator for many horses and is useful in specific training situations (see table opposite).

Some people are against using food at all, because horses that are fed from the hand often learn to 'mug' people. The key is to use food as a clear response to a desired behaviour. Avoid giving titbits the rest of the time.

## Voice

We generally overuse our voices around horses (see page 50). There are actually two ways in which the horse may understand the voice.

**1 Understanding the specific meaning of a word.** Taking the phrase 'good boy' as an example, in order for the word 'good' to mean anything to the horse it must be taught in conjunction with rewards that are more easily understood — for example, relaxation, petting or food. Once learned, the word or phrase can then be applied in many situations.

**2 Understanding tone.** This probably comes from the attitude of the person speaking: when we speak soothingly, we are normally relaxed; when we speak harshly, we are usually tense. So, if we say 'It's OK, there's nothing to worry about, *don't panic, don't panic, DON'T PANIC, GOOD BOY!!*' the meaning of the words is actually 'Yes, panic!'

## Petting

Horses use grooming behaviour to cement relationships, and if a horse wants his withers to be scratched he needs to approach the other horse in a friendly way. Horses that are used to humans will enjoy been stroked, scratched and rubbed, and respond to considerate petting much as they would to another horse. Horses do *not* generally enjoy being patted – they learn to live with it. If you want to test this, go and pat a human friend and see what sort of reaction you get.

## Effect of Rewards

| Reward | Example | Pros | Cons |
|---|---|---|---|
| **Relaxation** | When an excited horse has stopped dancing around and is standing still | • Easily understood by the horse | • Will not work if the horse is very wound up |
| **Food** | Getting a horse to allow medical treatment | • Very strong motivator<br>• Effective in making a positive association to replace a negative one | • If not given at the right moment, the horse may begin to pester for food |
| **Voice** | Long reining | • Can be used at any time<br>• 'Hands free', so can be used with the horse at a distance | • Tone and delivery may not be consistent<br>• Horse must have been taught the word<br>• Handler must have good timing<br>• If the horse associates soothing tones with tense situations, the voice may have the reverse effect to that intended |
| **Petting (stroking, rubbing or scratching)** | When riding, gently scratching the withers when a horse passes an object of which he is frightened | • Easy to use | • Horse must enjoy human touch<br>• Horse must be close enough |

## Learning in Natural and Domestic Situations

In Chapter 1 we briefly saw how a foal learns about his world in a natural and a domestic situation (see pages 10 and 14–15). Compared to feral horses, domestic horses generally live in a world of deprivation. This reduces their ability to make discoveries and choices. So, by the time we start working with a three-year-old, we may have an animal that has not developed his capacity to learn very far at all.

In contrast, by the time a feral horse is three years old he will have absorbed much of the wisdom held within the herd. He will know his home range, and where to find water and food. He will have learned horse language and be able to assess the character of other horses he may meet. Physically, he will have

---

■ **Learning on the job/1**

Relaxed and confident, this foal will not need much training when the time comes, having learned about the sights and sounds of the job as part of her early world.

## What is the Horse Teaching Us?

If a horse performs an action and achieves a pleasurable outcome, he will quickly learn that the action is useful. So, a horse that nuzzles your pocket and is rewarded with a handful of food will take to nuzzling everybody's pockets. A horse that knows that he gets attention when he kicks the stable door will quickly teach us to come and give him attention by kicking the stable door.

The best solution to this type of behaviour is for everyone to ignore it at all times. If anyone gives an occasional titbit, or sometimes approaches the horse when he kicks the door, that will encourage the behaviour. In the case of attention seeking through door kicking, some people report that a well-aimed dandy brush hitting the door when the horse kicks, or a shout, will soon stop the behaviour. Not kicking can be reinforced by approaching the horse when he has stopped kicking.

learned how to use his body, having been free to play and chase, and he will also have built up his stamina, covering long distances every day in search of food and water. Where seasonal migration takes place, the young horse will have travelled between summer and winter ranges. Importantly, he will have learned to make assessments of what is truly dangerous and what is not. In short, such a youngster will be equipped with all he needs in order to go out into the world and survive.

Horses that have been raised in this way learn incredibly quickly. I worked with a two-year-old cob that had lived on a mountain. He was level-headed and smart, and was happily being long reined from a headcollar towing a cardboard box in under an hour.

## What can Horses Learn?

Horses are capable of learning a lot more than most of us ever try to teach them. There are some people who teach a wide range of words, tricks and highly refined aids to produce amazing movements. However, many of us do not give our horses credit for having learned anything and continue cueing them even when they know what they are doing, simply because we haven't noticed that they are carrying out actions automatically.

My horse knows how to position himself at every gate in the area; he knows which end the catch is, no matter what the direction from which he has approached it. I do not need to steer him through the process, although he often needs reminding that we have to close gates as well as open them. When the catch and hinges on one gate were reversed, it took a lot of persuasion to make him go to the other end of the gate to open it. A horse that is fit and co-ordinated will not need to practise a new exercise many times once he has understood the objective and learned the movement.

# Motivation

A horse is more likely to do what we ask if he is motivated to do so. Horses have different motivations, such as food, curiosity or the desire to stop. In difficult situations, a relationship of trust with the handler will be of great benefit, with the horse motivated to do something simply because the handler asks him to. However, there will still be times when a horse is not at all interested in what we are doing, so our best option is to insist on what we want, but not labour the point when we get it. The horse then learns that if he does what is asked, he can stop doing it sooner.

The table shows how the same motivation may lead to both desirable and undesirable behaviours.

## Motivation Effects

| Motivation | Positive | Negative |
|---|---|---|
| Food | • Encouraging the horse to load<br>• Teaching reward | • Stopping to eat while being ridden<br>• Expectation of titbits, leading to biting |
| Company | • Meeting up with other horses on rides to encourage the horse to leave home | • Refusing to leave the yard alone<br>• Gets agitated if left alone |
| Looking for a mate | • Using straw that smells of mares to encourage a colt or stallion to load | • Uncontrollable behaviour in a colt or stallion |
| Curiosity | • Walking and riding out<br>• Introducing new activities (eg jumping, obstacle courses) | • Horse being more interested in some novelty than what you want him to concentrate on |
| Physical movement | • Enjoyable exercise<br>• Jumping up and down banks and over ditches<br>• Galloping | • Hyperactive, uncontrollable horses that are overfed and underexercised |

# Arousal

In order to achieve anything with a horse, we have to have his attention. The two extremes on the scale of arousal are sleeping and fleeing. The diagram shows how to recognize the horse's state of arousal and whether he will be able to take notice of us. The aim is always to bring the level of arousal to near the optimum before trying to do anything with a horse.

We must also consider our own state of arousal, as this may have a positive or negative effect on the horse. Generally, the more aroused we become, the more aroused the horse will become, as it is natural for him to respond to the arousal of other animals, be they peers or predators.

An animal that is tense cannot learn. Tension is the biggest obstacle to success in teaching. Tension may be labelled 'dominance', 'resistance', 'stubbornness' or 'defensiveness', but each of these terms is a value-judgment that blames the horse. We must always aim for relaxation and attentiveness, upping the level of enthusiasm depending on the task at hand. A high head, tight mouth and fixed eye are indicators of tension.

A horse will usually relax if you relax. Calming gestures are common to many species and your horse will respond to such gestures from you. Averting your eyes, turning your head or body to one side, relaxing your shoulders, resting one foot, breathing out and even chewing are all actions that horses recognize and understand. Similarly, being more energetic in your movements will make an unresponsive horse wake up.

■ **Conditions for optimal learning**
As the horse becomes increasingly aroused it will be impossible to teach him anything – but that does not mean that the horse is not learning. In fact, he is learning that this person/situation/place is dangerous and he will remember this for next time.

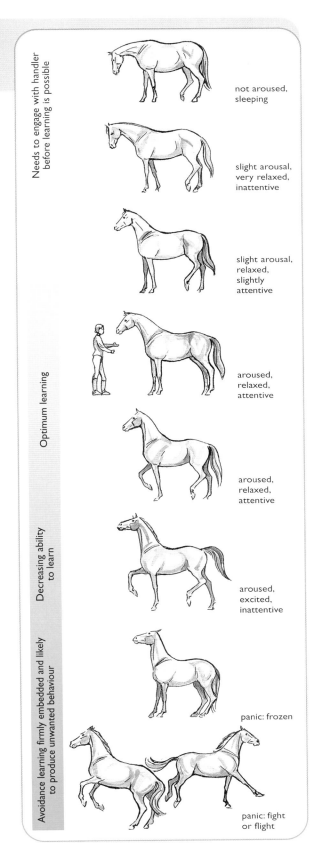

Needs to engage with handler before learning is possible

not aroused, sleeping

slight arousal, very relaxed, inattentive

slight arousal, relaxed, slightly attentive

Optimum learning

aroused, relaxed, attentive

aroused, relaxed, attentive

Decreasing ability to learn

aroused, excited, inattentive

Avoidance learning firmly embedded and likely to produce unwanted behaviour

panic: frozen

panic: fight or flight

# Building a Relationship with Your Horse

Many horses have a very low opinion of human beings and they prefer not to be in our company. Yet a young foal is usually interested in people, as are two- and three-year-olds that have not been upset in any way. What is it that we do to them to change them from friendly and inquisitive to switched off and unresponsive?

A typical interaction with a horse begins with the arrival of the rider. The horse is caught from the field or taken out of the stable, groomed briskly, tacked up, then schooled or hacked out for an hour. The human then goes away until the next time. What associations does the horse make from this interaction? To build a more friendly relationship, we can spend time with the horse that is more satisfying to him.

At the heart of the philosophy for working with a horse in a non-domineering way is the belief that the horse may actually choose to be with us and enjoy doing things with us. This is a break with most traditional thinking, in which restraint is at the heart of training horses. This has mainly come about because we make ourselves so unpleasant that they head off at the first opportunity. So what are the options for working with horses? Whatever the stage of training a horse is at, from untouched to highly trained, one or more of the ideas and activities presented on page 114–116 can be used.

## Setting the Ground Rules

The first time you gain a horse's attention and set a boundary that he understands, you have laid a foundation. This, combined with trust, will make rela-

### ■ The patient approach to training

The pony in this photograph was traumatized. Having lived wild for five years he was captured, gelded, loaded into a trailer and put into a tiny stable with two other ponies. His fear of humans had been compounded by the fact that no work had been done with him for three months. Here, the girl is simply ignoring him while offering fresh grass as an incentive to approach. He is engaged in an internal battle about whether he can risk approaching the human in order to get the grass. Any action taken to approach this pony would be counterproductive. Horses that are this afraid are some of the hardest to bring round.

tions run more smoothly. This is *not* the same as showing your dominance over the horse. It can be as simple as walking to the stable door and asking the horse to step back to allow you in. This can be done in a number of ways, depending on what the horse knows. If he is threatening to rush over you as you open the door, shaking a plastic bag over the door may work; gently pushing your thumb into the chest is effective on a horse that has no understanding of what you are asking. You have said 'Hi, I'm here, now please make room for me.' The horse is then aware that you have personal body space, just like another horse; *and* you have clearly indicated what you want and the horse has responded.

This setting of a ground rule may come at another time. It might take an hour to persuade a horse to walk over a drainage pipe across a bridleway, but the act of insisting and persisting for an hour, followed by a positive outcome – that is, nothing bad happening and plenty of praise – means that the next time will be much easier. A fight may be quicker in the short term, but provides a poor foundation for your future relationship.

The earlier we can set that limit both in the horse's life and in our individual relationship the better. Thoroughly handling a foal in the first few weeks and establishing that biting is not acceptable, that you have a personal space, and that you need to be able to touch him all over and lift his feet, may be all you need to do. You can then leave the foal alone so that he is not overfamiliar, and come back to him later knowing that he will have remembered those few rules you established right at the beginning.

## Approaching a Horse

Rushing up and patting or stroking a horse is the equivalent of a strange horse charging up and starting to groom another horse without any introduction. It is another example of how horses learn to

## Too Much Kindness

Being too nice to a horse because we want him to love us does not do him any favours. A horse that is never given any ground rules may become difficult to handle, because he has never been told what the acceptable limits of his behaviour are. Similarly, over the years we will come across new situations that require new rules, and a horse that understands the concept of ground rules will respond positively.

tolerate our poor understanding of horse language.

Horses exchange breath when they meet, an action that animal trainer Barbara Woodhouse was derided for imitating. However, it is a better way to greet a horse than by extending a hand – providing you can recognize horse signals. Many horses find being blown at almost irresistible, just as it is hard for us not to take a hand offered for shaking. However, a breath exchange between horses may well be followed up by a squeal and foreleg strike or a nip, so take care with a strange horse. Allowing the horse to sniff you up and down is probably a safer way of introducing yourself.

## Just Visiting

Visiting horses in the field just to say hello is an excellent way of keeping them sweet about your arrival, because they will not associate you with being taken away from their companions and exercised. The horses may simply ignore you and carry on grazing, or sniff you and then carry on, but the fact that you arrive, don't do anything to them, and then go will help in your relationship.

A horse that is difficult to catch will improve if he is not caught every time you appear. A titbit may be helpful in these cases, but it is best to keep food out of the process if possible. It is interesting to enter the field, then sit down on a wall or fence and ignore the horse. He will often graze his way up to you, have a sniff, and then leave.

## Grooming as Bonding

When horses groom each other, they generally do so along the neck, withers and back. Horses will also give their chests, undersides and rumps a good scratch on fences, stable walls and the ground. Horses do not allow each other to groom ticklish underbellies, legs or heads (although they will scratch their own). A horse shows his enjoyment of grooming by extending and wiggling his top lip, which is a precursor to scratching another horse's back.

Try grooming your horse without tying him up. The point of this activity is that nothing is demanded of the horse, the grooming is enjoyable and the horse is not worked afterwards. In this situation we have to be responsive to the signals the horse is giving us, enabling us to find out what he likes and dislikes, because he can choose to remain with us or not. Experiment with different brushes. Only groom the areas that the horse enjoys having groomed. The first time you may only manage to scratch his neck for a short time.

Once the horse finds being groomed pleasurable, you should be able to move on to grooming more ticklish areas, particularly if you choose soft brushes and work gently.

## Riding Out

In Chapter 10 we look at how to make riding more pleasurable for horses. Other strategies to give a positive outcome to riding are to explore new places, meet up with other riders, and to go visiting people. Visiting on horseback gives the horse a chance to stop and have a graze, so the purpose of the outing is

to go somewhere to eat. What could be more natural? Horses that are doing a specific job — for example, delivering milk or rounding up stock — rather than just performing exercises for the sake of it, learn the cues and aids associated with the activity and appear to enjoy their 'work'.

There is no point rewarding a horse with a bucket on his return from riding: all this does is make him rush home. He does not understand that the food means 'Thank you'. If you give a horse a titbit once you have untacked, all you are doing is rewarding the horse for standing in the stable. It is far better to turn out the horse in the field to have a roll and a stretch and return to eating with his friends.

## Exercises

To stave off boredom, instead of schooling or lungeing why not put up an obstacle course in the manège and work around it, either on the horse or leading from the ground? Riding over poles and weaving in and out of obstacles are good exercises for both horse

■ **Preparation**
Examining and walking over boards is good preparation for activities such as loading and crossing bridges.

and rider. Try doing exercises from the ground or teaching your horse tricks. These will keep both you and the horse interested, and your horse's powers of learning will amaze you.

## Eating Out

Taking a horse out on a long rope for a graze is especially good for stable-kept horses. It is also relaxing. If you are busy and do not have the time to ride, 15 minutes spent sitting with your horse while he munches the grass is quality time.

## Walking Out

Walking with a young horse to explore the world is a wonderful way of getting him to want to be with you. It builds on the animal's natural curiosity and his desire to follow. It is stimulating and will pay dividends once you begin to ride, because the horse is familiar with the outside world. It also allows you to watch your horse's reactions and learn more about his character.

To begin with it may help to lead from the front, as this is the natural way that horses follow each other – if they are unsure, they will actually step into each other's hoofprints. However, being safe when leading from in front depends on the horse already having been taught about not invading your personal space, and having a long enough rope to give yourself a 'buffer zone'. This gives the horse room to run forward if he is startled, then stop and turn to look at the source of alarm. For the horse to build confidence in the handler, he must not be held tightly when alarmed, but should be given the space to move and look so that he can satisfy his curiosity – an ordinary lead rope is not long enough to allow for this. Once you are established as the confident leader, the horse will depend on you when something frightens him, gluing himself to you when

■ **Providing variety**
Horses can be introduced to activities and obstacles in training that will keep them interested and improve their physical and mental development.

startled but without invading your personal space. *If you do not trust your horse not to run into you if he is frightened, walk in front but to one side.*

As the horse becomes more confident, instead of leading from the front you can drop back to his shoulder and let him take the lead. This is excellent preparation for when you start to ride him out.

■ **Early training**
This young Arab, being long-lined by trainer Mark Rashid, is learning to respond to the trainer and to pressure. He is turning beautifully, and beginning to bring his hindlegs under him. He is now perfectly familiar with ropes around him and on the ground, which will reduce the chances of accidents throughout his life.

## Working with Long Lines

Working on long ropes or reins is not necessarily the same as classical lunging. Some lunging techniques depend on a *lack* of togetherness: the horse is not allowed to approach and be with the handler, but instead has to keep going round in circles apparently just for the sake of it. In lieu of an enclosed space in which to work, a long line gives the opportunity for the horse to have freedom to move away to a certain distance, but ultimately keeps him with the handler.

Voice aids, gestures and touching cues can all be taught on long lines – for example, asking the horse to move sideways away from you in preparation for yielding to the aids from the legs.

## The Round Pen

Most people do not have access to a round pen, but the work done in one can be carried out by sectioning off a schooling area and putting something across the corners or making a ring from fencing tape, provided the horse is not likely to jump or barge out.

Round-pen techniques vary from practitioner to practitioner, but if used humanely give the horse the say over whether he wants to stick with us, and give us the ability to make being with us more comfortable than not. So, what goes on in the pen?

Initially, the horse responds to the strange situation, and sometimes to the attention of the handler, by going into flight mode. Some trainers actively drive the horse away. When nothing bad happens, the horse begins to relax and tire, often lowering his head, slowing down and relaxing the jaw. When the handler turns away, or steps backwards and bends down, the horse usually turns towards them to see what the source of his alarm actually is – this is exactly what a horse does when he has been startled. Once the horse has established that nothing bad is going to happen, having been welcomed by the handler his natural desire for company makes him stay with the person and accept what follows. Backing and riding a horse in a round pen – sometimes in a very short time – is successful because, after the initial sending away, the horse is kept relaxed at all times.

The round pen is not intrinsically humane and some horses may find it frightening. This is especially true if a lot of pressure is applied by the trainer, and the horse is sent away so much that he becomes exhausted. Care needs to be taken with horses that switch on to 'automatic pilot' and trot round and round with no sign of stopping. A horse that is not relaxing may need a different approach – for example, long hours spent sitting with him and encouraging contact.

# 8 Approaching Difficult Behaviour

*'I haven't failed, I've found 10,000 ways that don't work.'* Thomas Edison

The focus of this book is on how our behaviour affects our horses. Our treatment of them sometimes leads them to behave in ways that we find difficult to cope with. I use the term 'difficult behaviour' rather than 'misbehaviour', 'disobedience' or 'vice'. Horses do not enjoy being upset, frightened or hurt, so usually the horse's difficult behaviour causes the horse as many problems as the human. Horses do not enjoy fighting with us or wanting to run away. They tend to look for peace – if we allow them the opportunity.

# Analyzing Behaviour

## Overview

In addressing difficult behaviour, there are two aspects to consider. First, the source of the problem. Second, the problem in the moment that it occurs. However, to begin with it is important to take a holistic look at the horse's life.

### 1 Physical factors

The first consideration is the physical state of the horse. A veterinary examination should detect lameness or other problems, and there are now qualified equine physical therapists and dentists who can help diagnose problems. But we also have to consider difficulties that may only arise when a horse is wearing tack or carrying a rider, so we need to extend our examination of the horse to watching him in his own time, unencumbered by tack and rider. How does he move when free? Does he always strike off into canter on the same leg? When he rolls, does he always roll on one side only? How does he get up after lying down? Does he always rest the same leg?

If back problems are suspected, then maybe the saddle does not fit properly. If this is the case, perhaps the horse can be ridden bareback to see if the problem occurs (this may not be safe if the problem is manifesting itself as bucking). Remember that a back that has been damaged by a saddle may take time to heal, so simply changing to a better-fitting saddle may not solve the problem immediately.

Is discomfort in the mouth the problem? The horse can be ridden in a headcollar or hackamore to see if the behaviour still occurs when there is no bit. Is it the rider's handling? Someone calmer or with better hands can try the horse. Is it something as simple as the horse having a sharp tooth?

Undetected illness or injury may make a horse behave differently, so any changes in character or personality need to be investigated. A horse that is uncharacteristically aggressive or irritable may be ill. A horse that is lethargic or withdrawn may not be lazy but unwell.

### 2 The horse's life

In Chapter 1 we considered the three things that a horse needs in order to be satisfied: time to forage, companionship and space to move. Are these needs being met? Many problems arise from a horse having too much energy. Is his diet suitable? The horse's digestive system is designed to extract most of his energy from forage, not from sugar and grain. Most horses need little more than good-quality forage, with attention paid to the limitations that a restricted choice of pasture or dried forage may place on available nutrients. There is evidence that molassed feeds and high-grain diets give a feeling much like a runner's high, and stereotyped behaviour sometimes increases after a high-sugar feed.

A horse that is kept outside for most of the time and does not receive concentrated feed will reach a balance of energy, because he can burn off any high spirits through movement. That is not to say that a fit horse will not be full of himself at times, but he should not be jumping out of his skin due to pent-up energy. Trying to burn off a horse's energy of by lunging, for example, may simply have the effect of making the horse fitter than his rider.

### 3 The horse's history

A horse is not born with behavioural problems. The difficulties arise in response to events in his life. Therefore, if we know what has happened to a horse, we can often have a good insight into why he behaves in a certain way. For example, if we know that a horse has been roughly handled by a farrier, we will understand his reluctance to be shod.

Although we have to deal with the behaviour of the horse in the moment, knowing the horse's history will help us to avoid potentially dangerous situations. For example, with an ex-racehorse it might be a good idea at the beginning to avoid riding him in a large field with post-and-rail fencing, as this could act as a signal that a full-speed gallop is required!

Horses have strong individual personalities that influence the way they react to events. Behaviour is therefore a product of both genetics and experience. In response to this, our approach has to vary. One horse may react to nervous handling by becoming more determined in his actions, in an attempt to stamp some certainty on the situation; another may become nervous himself.

## 4 What the horse knows

We presume a lot about what horses know, but it may be that a horse is behaving in a certain way because he has not been taught any different. For example, horses need to be taught to stand still – there is a difference between being held still and actually standing still. A horse may never have been taught to be caught. A horse may not have been taught to wait while being mounted, and may understand the opposite – that the rider wants the horse to move off.

## Detailed Analysis

Simply put, a detailed analysis of the problem aims to answer the question of why the horse is doing what he is doing. It may seem impossible to answer this if a horse's history is unknown, but animals often unintentionally communicate what is troubling them. For example, if we note that a horse is terrified of a person holding a rope, we may watch more carefully

## Playing or Playing Up?

The words 'He's not really scared' are often followed by 'He's just trying it on.' It is true that a horse may peep and snort at a thing he is not really scared of, but the behaviour is better looked at as play, rather than an attempt to upset us.

Play is a rehearsal for real situations, and horses play at being frightened and rehearse what they would do if that boulder really were a lion. A horse that is playing at being scared will generally be more relaxed and willing to go forward after a moment's consideration. A genuinely frightened horse will be tense and is likely to seize up or run if forced to face the danger. Our reaction to the play determines the outcome of the behaviour. So, a horse that is prancing along in mock alarm at a plastic bag can be dealt with in three ways:

❍ Tell the horse that this is not time to play by making him refocus on the job at hand – in this case, asking the horse to walk and calm down.

❍ Join in with the game by encouraging the prancing and settling back down when you or the horse is ready.

❍ Seize up in fear or punish the horse, with the result that the plastic bag becomes genuinely dangerous because you have said it is.

Obviously, the third option will not help with the behaviour. If you know your horse well, option two is fun, but you must know the limits of his play reaction. If he likes to escalate into running away, try using the first tactic. Similarly, with a horse you don't know the best approach is to discourage the behaviour in a relaxed, non-threatening way.

Energetic play, such as bucking, is best dealt with by allowing the horse to run off steam at liberty. Once the excess energy has gone, he will be more amenable to going steadily.

and see that the horse is not afraid ropes or hands *per se*, but of a combination of the two. This may suggest that the horse had been beaten with a rope.

It is important to avoid simplistic, anthropomorphic explanations for behaviour. To dismiss a horse as 'dominant', 'ignorant', 'bad mannered' or 'bolshy' does not help in planning approaches to changing difficult behaviour. These may be our interpretations of the behaviour we see in human terms, but they do not explain where the behaviour comes from. They also put us in the position of accepting the behaviour because 'that is just the way he is'.

To analyse the problem, we need to consider the following aspects:

**Natural root** What is the purpose of the behaviour? What motivates the horse to perform it? Is it part of the flight reaction? Is it rooted in social behaviour?

**Situation** When does the horse perform the behaviour? Being ridden, being led, at a particular place, on a windy day, with a particular person, in the stable, when travelling, when a certain horse is present?

**Trigger** What happens immediately before the behaviour occurs? This may be very obvious (for example, a tractor approaching) or very subtle (the rider holding their breath in anticipation of a tractor approaching).

**History** Has the horse always done this? Has he been taught to do it? Has he been frightened in the past? Has he been trained with understanding?

**Horse's motivation** Is the horse afraid, in pain, feeling playful, over-energetic, bored, tired?

**Handler's reaction to the horse** Does the handler panic, shout, relax, try to reassure the horse, hit the horse, burst into tears?

**Horse's reaction to the handler** Does the horse become more frightened, relax, follow the handler, try to escape?

Watching, thinking and testing different hypotheses will lead to more understanding of the behaviour and can eventually solve the problem rather than just containing it. What actually triggers a horse that is being loaded to stop and resist? Is it because a horse-box is being used instead of a trailer? Is it the moment that people close in on the horse from behind to apply pressure? Is it the first foot on the ramp? Is it when pressure is applied to the headcollar?

Observing the horse when he is free with other horses may give us clues as to the source of a problem. A horse that prefers to follow the lead of another may not feel comfortable leading a ride at the beginning of his training and may always prefer to go behind. To ride such a horse on his own could require a lot of trust between the horse and handler – and probably a lot of footwork on the part of the latter.

When the history of a horse is known, it is often very clear why behaviour occurs. Horses that were violently branded the first time they came into contact with people show this clearly. Many will not allow a person to approach the area of the body where they were branded; they may even refuse to allow people to approach them on that side at all. It is worth bearing in mind that a history relayed by an owner is often coloured for all sorts of reasons, ranging from embarrassment to a lack of understanding of what is happening. It often tells us more about the speaker than the horse: what is one person's idea of a horse showing affection may be someone else's idea of being bitten.

Avoiding a fight is of the utmost importance when dealing with horses. Force in problem situations will simply reinforce the horse's upset and a fog of anger on our part makes it more difficult to analyse what is going on.

**■ Creating and resolving a problem** This sequence of photographs illustrates many of the elements discussed in this chapter. This filly has probably never been out of the pasture or left the group since she was born. The grey mare is probably her mother and the filly has been brought to the fair to be sold. At no point did the filly try either to kick in defence or attack the men. Horses that do attack have generally been pushed to the edge.

   The filly has been thrown on the ground in order to put a halter on her. This experience is about the most traumatic that a horse can have, because it mirrors being caught by predators. She has no idea that the men do not want to hurt her. As soon as she can, she rises, to find herself attached to shouting men, all focused on her. The filly's flight mechanism makes her try to escape, but she is prevented from doing so.

   In her panic, she jeopardizes her own safety, running backwards into the bales and chair. Notice the tension in the face of the grey mare. The filly freezes, waiting to see what will happen next. The men try another method. One pokes her with a stick, while another pulls her from in front. With her head raised in alarm and her attention on what is happening behind her, she is not going to move

   The men try towing her from the other horse. Again, the position of her head and her attention on the man behind her make it physically impossible for her to move. A moment of relaxation. With everyone's attention off her, the filly pricks her ears and looks towards the other horse. Ignoring a horse is a very powerful tool to reduce her tension. Finally, the men back off and let her simply follow the mare, which she does willingly. She would have done this from the outset had she not been thrown on the ground and terrified.

APPROACHING DIFFICULT BEHAVIOUR

# Changing Behaviour

All mammals are 'wired up' in basically the same way. Behaviour is a product of physiological processes. A lot of learning takes place in predictable ways, which means that we can teach all horses certain things and by and large they are programmed to respond in the same way. Beyond this, there will be individual responses and these vary between horses. For example, an experiment using positive reinforcement to retrain mares that wouldn't load resulted in five of the six mares entering a trailer, by training them to follow a wooden target that they had been taught to touch by giving a reward each time they touched it. The sixth mare got so far following the target, but then would only enter the trailer if another horse was led in first.

We should exercise caution in applying purely mechanistic training methods – for example, round-penning every horse. The animal's experiences of humans will influence how he reacts, so rather than use the same method with every horse it is important to examine various ways to teach them. To illustrate: the round-pen method of starting a horse may be fine with a confident youngster, but a horse that is frightened of humans will find the experience of being so close to a human terrifying in itself.

## Step by Step

Many problems can be resolved by breaking them down into stages, rewarding each stage, then building up step by step to the behaviour we require. This is the way we introduce new activities to any horse, but in the case of a horse that has learned that something is dangerous or frightening, the steps may need to be smaller and the time taken longer. To do this, we need to recognize any move in the direction we want. It may be very subtle, such as the horse moving one ear in the direction of the trainer or a slight increase in speed when asking for a transition. The point is that the slightest tendency towards the behaviour we want is rewarded. So we do not start out by asking for the whole behaviour immediately, but work on building up what we ask of the horse.

## Take Care

In addition to traditional devices of control, there are many new ones on the market. Make a careful assessment of so-called humane training tools such as pressure halters.

Such equipment applies more force than an ordinary halter or headcollar and it is possible to harm the horse inadvertently.

Halters with metal studs and those that tighten across the poll or block airways can cause great discomfort and pain. Halters that apply pressure through thin rope or knots should be avoided for general use.

## Time to Change

Horses that have problem behaviours may take a long time to change. Although some progress may be seen immediately, change continues over months and even years if the behaviour is deeply ingrained. It may take a few months for a horse to settle into a new home and get used to new companions, so it is often worth giving a troubled horse time to 'chill out' and calm down before starting to work with him.

## Attention Forward

To achieve anything, we need the horse to have his attention on the task, yet much of the time we distract the horse. There are many situations in which a horse will not want to go forward and our reaction is often to begin hitting, kicking, yelling or flapping at the horse. The effect of this is to divert the horse's attention from the front (where we need it) to what is going on behind.

When loading a reluctant horse, for example, the usual course of action is for people to approach the horse from the rear, converging on him with whips, flapping arms and lunge lines to put around his rump. Is it any wonder that the horse, caught between his fear of what is in front and his concern about what is going on behind, begins to panic and resist? The same is true of crossing ditches, walking

**■ Divided attention**
The ear positions of this horse show that he is concentrating on two different things at once – and they say horses aren't clever!

through water and passing unfamiliar objects. Given time and no distraction, most horses will eventually go forward, provided their attention is kept in the direction you want to go.

## Letting It Go

There is no point in tackling behaviour just for the sake of it. There are some behaviours that are best left alone, and if there is an easier way to do something that achieves the same end then it is worth going for. An example would be a horse that does not like being hosed down. A bucket of warm water and a sponge will achieve the desired result of cleaning sweat off the horse with no unnecessary fuss.

### The Brain-Injured Horse

A horse that has damage to his brain resulting in unpredictable behaviour may be impossible to change. If a part of the brain is damaged so that it can no longer function, no amount of re-education will help. A positive diagnosis is impossible without high-tech scanning techniques, but behaviours that may give cause for concern would be inexplicable actions that are not dependent on the situation – for example, sudden bolting either in the field or when being ridden. The suspect horse may be the only one in a grazing group acting in that way.

A horse with brain damage may be able to have a life as a companion animal, or as a brood mare if the injury was acquired rather than inherited. The uses that such a horse is put to will, of course, depend on how the injury manifests itself. For example, a horse that has staggering fits is not safe to ride.

# Case Study: Too Much, Too Young

As a four-year-old Tom had already won a considerable amount of prize money for showjumping. He was then sold to a competent, talented young rider, who went on to win a leading junior showjumping title. Tom continued to win competitions, and eventually changed hands for the princely sum of £15,000.

> 'As a result, the decision was taken to shoot him, but at the last moment he was turned away to calm down.'

The problem for Tom was that, having been brought on too fast, he was only eligible to jump in big classes. He was sold to a less able rider who did not give him confidence, and he began to refuse. Tom was sent away to be 'straightened out'. It appears that extreme methods were used and he retaliated with aggression. On one occasion, six men pushed him up against a wall in an unsuccessful attempt to get his rider on board; another time he attacked a child who had fallen off him. As a result, the decision was taken to shoot him, but at the last moment he was turned away to calm down.

---

■ **Tom (above)**

In the first photograph, Tom is approaching the photographer who is holding a slice of hay. His reaction springs from fear that the food will be taken away from him and he never follows up the threatening expression with any attack. The hungrier he is, the more frantic he gets. It is possible that at some time in his life Tom had to compete with other horses for limited food. Note the reaction of the other horse.

In the next we see Tom's reaction to a handler approaching with headcollar or tack. The negative association he has with the arrival of tackle causes him to make it impossible to approach his head. Pressure from the handler may result in a tail swish or a threat to kick. He can be brought round with food, or by gently swinging a rope towards his quarters. A domineering approach simply makes him more resistant.

Bareback and with a bitless bridle, Tom is relaxed and willing. Contrast his expression to that in the photo on page 83.

# A second chance

His present owners bought him without knowing this story, although they noticed that he had 'gone in the eyes'. Three months later they were informed how dangerous the pony was, but having had no incidents in this time, they got on with jumping. Tom's hatred of this was clear: every fence was taken with ears pinned back and mouth tight. However, Tom trusted his new rider and they were very successful.

Evidence of the abuse Tom had suffered was plain. His nose bore a thin, white scar where wire had been used to slow him down. The sound of a whip sent him into a panic. Any sign of anger in his rider and he would try to run away. His owners worked with him without violence. They trained him to stop cow-kicking when mounted by giving him a titbit as the child was legged up. When I first saw him, he became extremely hyped up when expecting food, frantically nipping and pulling faces. When I moved around him, he swished his tail.

Aged 19, it was time for Tom to retire and I offered to take him on loan. When he arrived, I turned him out full time with two other geldings. As he had been aggressive to people in the past, my approach was to let him relax and not pressure him. He was aggressive around food, suggesting that at some time he had had to compete with other horses for it. To stop him harassing me and threatening the other horses, I gave him no titbits or bucket feed. Within days he stopped nipping.

Tom's back and saddle were fine so I considered his bit, which was extremely severe because he had bolted a couple of times in the ring. As I had no plans to jump him, I started riding him in a milder bit plus a hackamore, until I was sure he would not bolt. I then dispensed with the bit altogether, and just rode him in the hackamore. This encouraged him to lower his head and lengthen his neck so that he could walk out better and climb hills. Having never been ridden out, he loved it, and marched ahead with his ears pricked. If he was uncertain, he would simply stand and wait. His habit of shaking his head in protest at being mounted vanished after two outings, helped by the fact that I dismounted and remounted on the ride (I have since found that he objects to anyone new mounting until he trusts them). It was evident that under the blustering exterior there was a nervous but sensible little horse.

After a couple of weeks Tom's only defensive behaviour was to stand with his head in the corner of the stable when I went to tack him up. I could have avoided the issue by tying him first, but I was interested to see whether he would change. I was sure he would kick if I tried to push him, so I left the saddle on the stable door as I went in and out. Sometimes he stood for a few minutes with his head in the corner, even when I wasn't around. Eventually he would turn round and come to the front of the stable, and I would wait a while and then take the tack away, without tacking up.

Tom is an example of a horse who has people figured out. He quite likes us, even though he has been treated so badly at times. He loves being turned out with his friends and acts more like a colt than a veteran. I hope that eventually he will give up diving into the corner of the loosebox when he sees his saddle, but I am sure that if he returns to a situation where he is mistreated and put under pressure, his difficult behaviour will return.

## Conclusions

Tom's problems arose from:

- Being brought on too fast, too young.
- Abusive training.

The solutions include:

- No violence.
- A less pressured life.
- Using a hackamore.

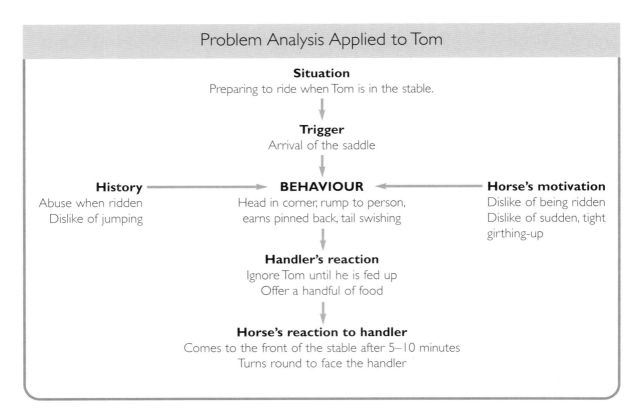

## Problem Analysis Applied to Tom

**Situation**
Preparing to ride when Tom is in the stable.

↓

**Trigger**
Arrival of the saddle

↓

**History** → **BEHAVIOUR** ← **Horse's motivation**

| History | BEHAVIOUR | Horse's motivation |
|---|---|---|
| Abuse when ridden<br>Dislike of jumping | Head in corner, rump to person,<br>earns pinned back, tail swishing | Dislike of being ridden<br>Dislike of sudden, tight<br>girthing-up |

↓

**Handler's reaction**
Ignore Tom until he is fed up
Offer a handful of food

↓

**Horse's reaction to handler**
Comes to the front of the stable after 5–10 minutes
Turns round to face the handler

# 9 Problems

*'Over and over again rodeo people stressed that the greatest percentage of bucking horses are "spoiled saddle horses", or "kids' horses" or riding mounts that "go sour".'*

Rodeo, *Elizabeth Atwood Lawrence*

It is difficult to provide solutions to problems without seeing what is happening. This chapter aims to give some pointers to understanding why problems arise and to suggest possible solutions. Every horse (and person) has an individual personality and individual experiences that will dictate behaviour, so the approach will vary in each specific case. It may be more effective to bring in an experienced person to help with a problem, not only because such a person has skills but also because fresh eyes can bring a new perspective. However, do make sure that the person works in a way with which you are comfortable: it's your horse, your money and you have valid opinions, too.

# Handling Problems

## Biting

The knack to dealing with biting is not to make the horse head-shy. Therefore, it is far more effective if you can make the horse think he has caused himself discomfort. Your reaction to biting has to be immediate and preferably should not involve your hands coming into view.

**NATURAL ROOT**
- Horse uses mouth to explore the world
- Playing
- Grooming

**NATURAL RESOLUTION**
- Other horses teach youngsters about appropriate force

**POSSIBLE CAUSES**
- Foal not taught that biting is not acceptable
- Horse is expecting titbits
- Horse is playing
- Horse is afraid and defending himself

**IMMEDIATE ACTION**
- Raise an elbow so the horse bangs into it, but don't actively throw the elbow
- Yell and make a fuss
- Pull whiskers
- Deliver a cupped-hand smack on the muzzle that makes a lot of noise but does not hurt

**LONG-TERM ACTION**
- Do not push and paw the horse's muzzle away – this mimics playing and will encourage the horse to bite
- Stop feeding titbits

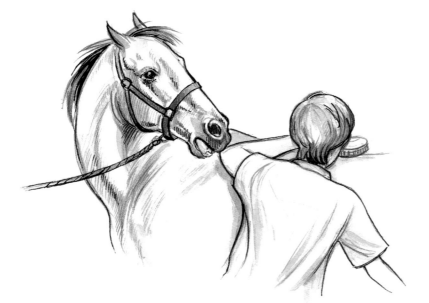

By chance, I discovered a useful tool for stopping a horse biting. I was wearing a hair clip that had a small pointed rod that looked like a thin pencil. I was holding the rod when a pony decided to nip my hand. He pricked himself on the point of the rod, pulled away, then came back to investigate again. After a few tries he decided it really wasn't worth it. All I had to do was hold the rod in a position that meant he would grab it.

# Kicking

Foals are born kicking and are taught not to kick by the other horses in the group, who do not tolerate being booted by upstart youngsters. Kicking is a horse's natural defence. A few will resort to it if they feel they have no alternative and are under threat from people. Some may then learn that it can get them out of certain situations.

## NATURAL ROOT

- Defence of body space
- Removal of flies or reaction to colic
- Fighting

## NATURAL RESOLUTION

- There is always space for horses to keep their distance

## POSSIBLE CAUSES

- Foal not taught that kicking is not acceptable
- Development of the action of pulling the leg away when being handled
- Proximity of other horses when being groomed
- Discomfort when being groomed
- Final defence against attack from humans

## IMMEDIATE ACTION

- With a foal, yell and jump in the air to startle him — he will soon give up.
- With a confirmed kicker, avoid being in a position to be kicked

## LONG-TERM ACTION

- Take pressure off in situations where the horse feels he has to defend himself
- Stand out of range and repeatedly touch the horse's leg with a piece of hosepipe or something similar until he is fed up with kicking
- Reward the horse for not kicking when touched
- Teach the horse always to turn his head towards you and his hindquarters away (see Difficult to Catch on page 131)

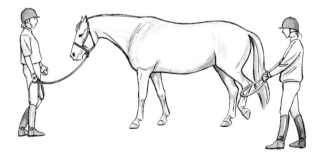

### ■ Training not to kick when touched

One handler holds the rope attached to the horse's headcollar and has some food ready to give as a reward. The other, standing out of range, holds a loop of hosepipe. The horse is touched with the hosepipe and is rewarded if he doesn't kick. He is not rewarded if he raises a leg.

When the horse is relaxed and accepting the hosepipe is placed round the leg and he is rewarded for not kicking.

Once progress is seen, the second handler can progress to touching the leg with a hand.

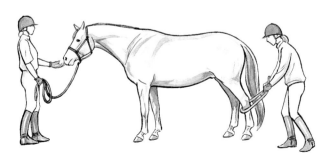

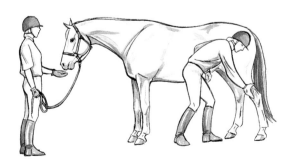

# Barging

Horses do not generally run people over, but there are many young horses around who do not understand about keeping an acceptable distance because they have never lived in a group of horses.

### NATURAL ROOT

- Foals push against their mothers
- Horses push each other out of the way

### NATURAL RESOLUTION

- Adult horses will not tolerate being barged

### POSSIBLE CAUSES

- Horse has a strong desire to go somewhere
- Horse does not understand personal space
- Humans move out of the way, so the behaviour is reinforced

### IMMEDIATE ACTION

- Make yourself big – yell, wave your arms at the horse's eye level
- If you are genuinely in danger, move

### LONG-TERM ACTION

- Exercises from the ground with the horse in hand
- Use a stick with a plastic bag on the end to make the horse go back

# Pulling Back When Tied

Horses have to learn that a rope attached to a wall or to a human means that they must stay put.

### NATURAL ROOT

- Does not occur

### NATURAL RESOLUTION

- None needed

### POSSIBLE CAUSES

- Horse has never been tied
- Horse has been tied up and then frightened
- Horse has learned that he can break ropes, string, headcollars

### SOLUTIONS

- Reteach the horse to be tied
- If the horse has a tendency to panic, do not tie him up but slip the rope through a fastener so that it can be pulled out

■ **Teaching to tie/1**
The aim is to prevent the horse panicking from pressure on the poll, *not* to let him fight it out against the rope. Use a thick, soft piece of fabric around the horse's neck and make sure that it cannot slide up or tighten. Attach the lead rope, and thread it through the headcollar. Tie it with a quick-release knot. Stay with the horse, reassuring him if he leans back, and be prepared to undo the knot if he panics. *Never try this with a horse that is known to panic.*

■ **Teaching to tie/2**
The handler holds the end of the rope to teach the horse to relax to tension. If the horse leans, the rope is tight. The horse can release the tension by stepping forward. If the horse panics the rope can be lengthened safely.

# Difficult to Catch

Young, unspoilt horses are usually interested in people and choose to approach. A horse that has taken to avoiding being caught will actually need to be taught to be caught.

Teaching a horse to be caught can be started in a small area, even a loosebox. The aim is that the horse learns to turn his head to you when you approach. A titbit may be an easy way to encourage this behaviour in a horse that has been handled, understands titbits and is not prone to biting, but if you do not want to use food then gently swinging a rope towards the horse's hindquarters will often have the same effect. You must stop swinging the rope as soon as the horse moves round. The size of the area can then be increased gradually – for example, to half a school, then the full school or a taped-off area in the field. Once the horse has learned always to turn to you when you approach, this behaviour should operate in the same way in the field. If this is combined with making time spent with you more enjoyable for the horse, catching will become less of a problem. *If you use food to catch your horse, be careful when entering a group of horses, as being trapped in the middle of a food-induced dispute is one of the most dangerous situations there is. Never carry a bucket into a group of horses.*

## NATURAL ROOT
- Moving away from anything worrying

## NATURAL RESOLUTION
- None needed

## POSSIBLE CAUSES
- Unpleasant experiences
- Boredom with activities

## IMMEDIATE ACTION
- Catch other horses and allow the difficult horse to follow them into the stable, corral or yard
- Persist until the horse gives up – this may be impossible due to lack of time and the size of the field

## LONG-TERM ACTION
- Take the horse out of the field to have a small feed, then turn him back out – he will learn to see your arrival as positive
- Teach the horse to be caught (see above)

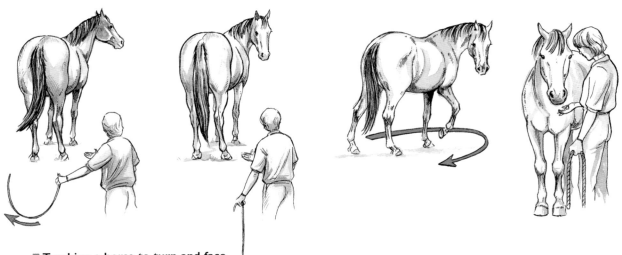

## ■ Teaching a horse to turn and face

Swing a rope underarm towards the haunch on the side you want the horse to turn away. Offer a hand, using food if the horse understands and responds to food rewards. When the horse turns his head, stop swinging the rope. Resume spinning if the horse turns away again. When the horse turns give a reward or a rub.

## ■ Advance–retreat method

'Advance–retreat' works with some horses. Each time the horse turns away, drive it further away; then, the moment he indicates a readiness to stop, turn away and retreat a couple of steps. The horse will often turn to look. Approach again. If horse moves away, repeat the first two steps. When the horse turns he may follow. When the horse is fully facing you, approach him from the side without focusing all your attention on him. The horse will usually accept being caught.

# Eating Problems

As explained in Chapter 1, horses are not designed to go for periods without food, or to have to compete for food. Unnatural feeding, both in terms of foodstuffs and feeding routines, leads to horses showing symptoms of what may described as eating disorders. These range from aggression around food to not eating enough.

Slow eating and loss of weight may be a sign of problems with the horse's teeth, so get them checked first. Also bear in mind that some horses have ulceration of the stomach lining and the pain may be exacerbated by high levels of sugar in the diet. Crib-biting after eating is a symptom of stomach problems. Horses on restricted grazing may gorge themselves when given the opportunity, so keep them topped up with hay in between bouts of grazing. A horse that is obsessed with food will be made worse by constant feeding of titbits.

**NATURAL ROOT**

- A fussy eater would die so is unlikely to exist
- Usually no competition for food

**NATURAL RESOLUTION**

- Not applicable

**POSSIBLE CAUSES**

- Unnatural feeding practices
- Long periods with no food
- Concentrated high-energy, molassed feeds
- Restricted access to food (eg laminitic horses)
- Competition and stress around food – the horse is unsettled and threatened

**SOLUTIONS**

- Alter the horse's lifestyle so that he becomes relaxed
- Give constant access to forage
- Make forage the main energy source
- Give space away from, but in sight of, other horses when feeding
- Do not leave the horse for long periods with no food

**FOR LOADING AND SHOEING PROBLEMS SEE CHAPTER 5.**

# Ridden Problems

## Blowing Out When Being Saddled

Horses blow out when being girthed up because they find it uncomfortable, not because they have plans to drop us in the mud. They brace against the pressure, sometimes lowering the head as well. Once they relax, the girth is then looser and the saddle slips. Perhaps if we still wore corsets we would be more sympathetic.

Let the girth right down and girth up loosely at first, just enough to hold the saddle in place. Take it up gently until it is tight enough to hold the saddle in place while mounting. Mount from a low wall or mounting block. Tighten the girth again once you are on board, if necessary. With time, the horse should stop associating girthing up with discomfort and the behaviour may disappear altogether.

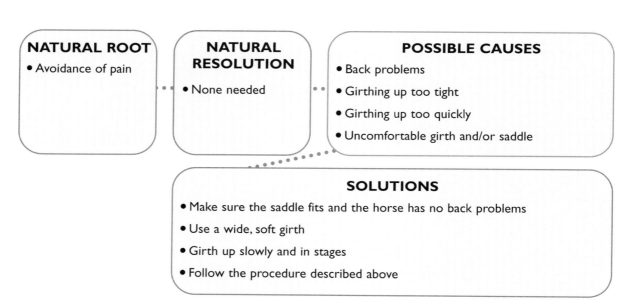

**NATURAL ROOT**
- Avoidance of pain

**NATURAL RESOLUTION**
- None needed

**POSSIBLE CAUSES**
- Back problems
- Girthing up too tight
- Girthing up too quickly
- Uncomfortable girth and/or saddle

**SOLUTIONS**
- Make sure the saddle fits and the horse has no back problems
- Use a wide, soft girth
- Girth up slowly and in stages
- Follow the procedure described above

## Napping: Jibbing, Shying, Turning Round, Backing Up

Horses that do not go forward confidently usually need training to build their confidence, as described in Chapter 7. If the horse is consistently refusing to go forward because he dislikes the activity – for example, he does not want to enter a show ring – it may be kinder to accept this and look for an alternative activity, or find a different horse.

Being herd-bound is the natural condition of the horse. Horses are born into groups and stay in them if possible. Teaching a horse to go out alone is part of his education and is essential, as if a horse will not leave the yard without another horse this limits the activities that can be undertaken.

In fact, we do not actually ask horses to go out alone: we are always with them, so we have to become worthy companions with whom to venture out. A bond of trust between you and your horse is the key. A young

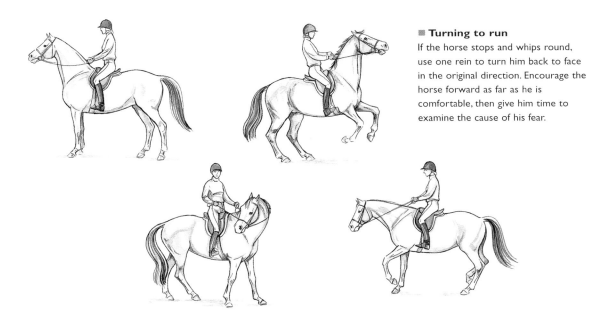

**■ Turning to run**
If the horse stops and whips round, use one rein to turn him back to face in the original direction. Encourage the horse forward as far as he is comfortable, then give him time to examine the cause of his fear.

horse that has been out with his mother as a foal will be less afraid. The years before starting are valuable for leading out and taking advantage of the curiosity of a young horse and his desire to explore.

An older horse with the problem can be encouraged away from home bit by bit and rewarded by simply going for a graze or meeting a friend somewhere along the route. Again, gentle persistence is important. Often the problem develops because people simply relent and never try to venture out alone. Occasionally, the root of the problem is that it is the rider who is afraid to go out alone and this apprehension is transmitted to the horse.

## NATURAL ROOT

- Caution when examining something
- Flight reaction

## NATURAL RESOLUTION

- Horse satisfies curiosity
- If there is danger, the horse runs away

## POSSIBLE CAUSES

- Problems with eyesight
- Rider preventing the horse from turning his head to look properly
- Strong dislike of an activity
- Fear of something in front
- Startled
- Conflict because the horse wants to stop but has learned he will be hit if he tries to, so he keeps moving but not in a forward direction
- Desire to stay with companions or fear of the outside world

## IMMEDIATE ACTION

- Allow the horse time and space to look
- If the horse turns round or backs up, if possible return him to where he started or at least get him facing the way you want and standing still
- Get off and lead

## LONG-TERM ACTION

- Always allow the horse time to examine objects to accustom him to his world
- Build the horse's confidence to go out alone by leading him out or riding out to meet other horses

# Running Away (Bolting)

There is a difference between a horse truly bolting in panic, and tanking off because he likes the feel of grass underfoot. However, both can be frightening to the rider and dangerous. Prevention of the latter depends on not always galloping a horse in the same place or on the same surface. Some horses that take off at a gallop have actually been taught to do so, commonly by fearless teenage riders.

When starting horses, it is a good idea not to introduce cantering or galloping too early. Wait until the horse understands the aids to slow down and stop, and is used to changes of weight in the saddle. This will prevent him becoming alarmed if you accidentally become unbalanced.

## NATURAL ROOT

- Flight reaction
- Play

## NATURAL RESOLUTION

- None needed

## POSSIBLE CAUSES

- Fear
- *Joie de vivre*
- Pain

## IMMEDIATE ACTION

- Do not haul on the reins – if the horse is running away from the pain of the bit, this will make it worse
- Use bodyweight and alternating pressure on one rein then the other to unbalance the horse
- Turn the horse on to a large circle, then decrease the arc
- If possible, run the horse uphill until he stops

## LONG-TERM ACTION

- Check that the horse is not in pain
- Do not resort to a more severe bit – sometimes the opposite may work as the horse loses his fear of the bit
- If the horse is fearful, build his confidence as described in Chapter 7

### ■ Effects of pulling on the reins

Horses can be taught to stop by using one rein, because once the horse turns his head his hindquarters will disengage. This can be taught when schooling, then used regularly when the horse shows signs of taking off. However, beware of using a one-rein stop when the horse is moving fast, because this can easily cause him to fall over.

brace

### ■ Two reins

Pulling on two reins gives the horse something to pull against and allows him to tense his jaw and neck. The discomfort in his mouth actually encourages him to pull more because he wants to run away from the pain.

### ■ One rein

Pressure on one rein breaks the brace and unbalances the horse so that he cannot lean and pull. The degree of pressure will depend on the situation, but generally only a small difference between the reins is sufficient to have an effect but not tip the horse.

# Headshaking, Shuffling and Jogging

Headshaking and tossing may be a health issue or due to dental problems, but it is also frequently a protest at the rider hanging on to the reins too tightly and making the horse uncomfortable, either through pain caused by the bit or because he finds it difficult to move when his head is restricted.

### NATURAL ROOT
- Removal of irritation

### NATURAL RESOLUTION
- None needed

### POSSIBLE CAUSES
- Usually due to tension on the reins causing discomfort in the horse's mouth, neck and back
- Health problems (may be seasonal, eg pollen allergy) – also seen when not ridden

### IMMEDIATE ACTION
- Lengthen the rein
- Check the ears, mouth, nose and eyes for obvious signs of irritation

### LONG-TERM ACTION
- Check the horse's teeth
- Learn to ride without pressure on the horse's mouth
- In schooling, improve the use of your hands
- Try different bits to find one that is more comfortable for the horse, or consider riding in a hackamore
- Nose nets seem to solve the problem for some horses

## Not Going Forward

I frequently see horses shuffling along at a snail's pace or jogging when hacking out. By 'jogging' I mean a bouncy up-and-down trot on the spot, not the smooth, ground-covering jog of the Western horse. These problems arise either from the rider's belief that the horse should be 'on the bit' all the time, or because the rider is fearful and clinging on to the reins. The effect is like driving a car with the handbrake on. These paces are uncomfortable for both horse and rider. We should be aiming for a horse that steps out freely, going forward in a relaxed manner with each stride swinging through to its full length and with the head free to move.

A horse that shuffles will have a side-to-side movement when viewed from in front because he has to swing his front end sideways to make room for the leg to come through. The jogger will often toss his head as he tries to get more rein and more freedom. Jogging may look showy but it is an inefficient pace, slower than a slow walk yet using more energy. It is uncomfortable for the rider and increases concussion to the horse's legs.

Shuffling can be solved by giving the horse more rein. A jogger needs to be brought back to a walk each time he jogs, then rewarded for each step of walk. With time, he will take more steps before breaking into a jog because he will find walking freely more comfortable.

# Bucking

Bucking is another of the earliest behaviours that foals engage in as they frolic around their mothers. It is the way horses try to remove unwanted beings from their backs. The process of starting a horse is in part to convince him that we are 'wanted' beings.

## NATURAL ROOT

- Removing a predator
- Playing
- Regaining balance

## NATURAL RESOLUTION

- None needed

## POSSIBLE CAUSES

- Back problems
- *Joie de vivre*
- Regaining balance
- Learned behaviour to remove the rider

## IMMEDIATE ACTION

- When warning signs of bucking appear, keep the horse's head up: tightening one rein prevents the horse bracing
- Turning the horse's head to one side can be effective
- When bucking occurs, lean back, push your heels down and tip the horse's nose from side to side to unbalance him and break the brace between his head and your hand

## LONG-TERM ACTION

- Check the horse's back for pain and make sure the saddle fits
- If the horse is frightened of the saddle, retrain
- Give the horse time to develop balance, and improve rider balance
- Avoid situations that induce bucking (eg holding the horse back behind other horses)
- If the horse has learnt he can remove a rider, he should be ridden by someone who can prevent the behaviour and/or stay on

■ **Riding the buck**
Lean back, brace against the stirrups with your heels down and tip the horse's nose from side to side by alternating pressure on each rein.

■ **Preventing the buck**
When the horse drops his head, tip the nose to one side.

# Rearing

Fortunately, few of us come into contact with horses that rear. Do not put yourself at risk – seek sympathetic expert help.

## NATURAL ROOT
- Playing
- Fighting
- Mating
- Protecting head

## NATURAL RESOLUTION
- None needed

## POSSIBLE CAUSES
- Often develops from napping
- Horse has the desire to escape but is prevented from fleeing
- Pain in the mouth and head

## IMMEDIATE ACTION
- Do not put pressure on the bit
- Lean forward – grab the horse's mane or neck as necessary, but leave the reins loose
- On landing, request that the horse faces forwards but allow him to take a few steps back, turn or stand still until calm
- Use the rein to turn the horse's head to one side, making it difficult for him to rear

## LONG-TERM ACTION
- Help the horse to face his fears – this can be done in hand
- Make the horse more comfortable in his mouth

Usually the final factor that causes a horse to rear is the rider pulling the reins. The horse is trying to move but the only direction open is up. Allowing him to back up or turn should avert a rear. Permitting the horse to move prevents escalation of the behaviour.

It is important to allow calm to be restored as soon as the threat of rearing has passed. For example, do not continue spinning him in circles. Return the horse to where the problem started and calmly request forward movement. The horse must learn that rearing does not achieve anything and peace can be found by not doing it. If the process of preventing the rear upsets the horse even more, the situation could get worse.

When leading, pulling a horse down will just give him something to pull against. A firm tug, release, then another tug on the rope to unbalance him is more effective, but don't pull him over onto you.

■ **Rearing**
Lean forward, grab the mane and leave the reins loose.

On landing, turn the horse in a full circle.

Return the horse to the starting position (or as close as is possible).

# Dislike of Going Through Water/ Over Unfamiliar Surfaces

Horses depend on their feet for survival. This means that they are naturally cautious about stepping into a place they cannot see or on to surfaces that are unfamiliar. *When offering a lead to horse who is worried about walking through or over an obstacle, give yourself plenty of room in case he decides to leap instead of walking. Position yourself so that the horse does not land on top of you.*

## NATURAL ROOT

- Horse cannot see what he is stepping in/on to

## NATURAL RESOLUTION

- Horse avoids putting his feet anywhere he does not trust
- Horse waits for another horse to lead the way

## POSSIBLE CAUSES

- Instinctive suspicion
- Rider prevents the horse from lowering his head to look at the water
- Bad experience, such as being forced into a bog by a rider

## IMMEDIATE ACTION

- Allow the horse to look
- Take your time
- Offer a lead by walking through or over first

## LONG-TERM ACTION

- Problem will resolve by carrying out the immediate action and gently insisting
- Use food as a reward
- Accept one foot in/on first time and build on that

# Eating While Ridden

A horse, or usually a pony, that constantly snatches at vegetation is uncomfortable to ride. In summer, vegetation is often at nose height, which is irresistible. Some ponies will actually stop and graze, ignoring all the rider's actions, which is a particular problem for children. Hitting the horse will simply make him grab the grass and then run. If anyone has found a failsafe way of stopping this behaviour, I would love to hear about it.

See Causes and Actions opposite.

### NATURAL ROOT

- Eating on the move is part of grazing behaviour

### NATURAL RESOLUTION

- None needed

### POSSIBLE CAUSES

- Natural behaviour
- Hunger, especially if the horse is on restricted rations
- Horse has learned that he can eat while ridden

### IMMEDIATE ACTION

- Hold one rein firm, so that the horse cannot brace against it (as he can against two)
- Use a grass rein, provided it does not impede the horse's head movement
- Fit a muzzle, provided it is comfortable
- Once the horse's head is down, do not haul on the reins – get him to walk on as he has to lift his head to do this

### LONG-TERM ACTION

- Teach a cue that means 'You can eat' (eg dropping the reins on the neck)
- Teach a cue that means 'Lift your head' (eg the word 'up' or a certain sound)

## Rolling While Ridden

Few horses roll when ridden, though I have known riding-school ponies that had discovered rolling as a short cut to removing an irritating child. Some horses roll, or threaten to, when in water.

### NATURAL ROOT

- Scratching back
- Removing sweat
- Need to cool down
- Getting a coating of mud/dust for protection from cold or insects

### NATURAL RESOLUTION

- None needed

### POSSIBLE CAUSES

- As natural root
- Horse has learned that he can remove the rider

### IMMEDIATE ACTION

- Get the horse moving by flapping and yelling
- If the horse goes down, dismount but continue kicking up a fuss to make the activity unrewarding
- With time, the horse will not find any enjoyment in the activity and should stop – if you are outraged enough the first time, he may not try again

### LONG-TERM ACTION

- Avoid getting into water or mud
- Do not get the horse too sweaty, and allow him time to cool down during exercise

# Stereotyped Behaviours

In Chapter 5 we examined the reasons for the behaviours commonly known as 'stable vices', which include weaving, boxwalking, crib-biting, windsucking, head bobbing and so on.

Traditionally, these have been dealt with by physical prevention and sometimes by causing the horse discomfort. However, these methods do not take away the underlying reason for the behaviour or remove the horse's desire to carry it out. It is thought that stereotyped behaviours actually help the horse deal with his situation – they are an outlet for the frustrations and stress that a horse is feeling.

Other treatments for stereotyped behaviours are surgical (operating) or chemical (drugs). Neither of these 'solutions' offers much hope for the horse, who still suffers the mental anguish that results from the lifestyle forced upon him yet has lost his only outlet – the ability to perform the behaviour. Surgery may involve, for example, removing parts of and nerves to muscles in the throat and neck to prevent crib-biting. Drugs related to those used in the treatment of human mental health problems often simply numb the emotions. They also have side effects, so it may not be to the horse's benefit to administer them, even if they appear to cure the problem.

Mirrors are now available to give the horse the belief that he has company and more space, but a horse is an intelligent, social animal, so a mirror is a poor substitute for real equine company. After all, you cannot mutually groom with a mirror.

The best solution is prevention:

❍ Give the horse a more natural lifestyle in the form of eating time, companionship and space.
❍ Do not subject him to high-stress situations, such as sudden weaning, or to long-term stress.
❍ Be sensitive to what the horse finds stressful. Some horses find competing difficult, some hate not to be able to see other horses.

A horse that already exhibits stereotyped behaviours will benefit from the suggestions above. Sometimes the behaviour will vanish altogether. However, once a behaviour is established it may be difficult to cure. In the most extreme cases, the horse will continue the behaviour even when turned out with company, although over time this may decrease. Horses that stop the behaviour when living more naturally may still perform it when placed back in the conditions that induced the problem in the first place. The only solution is a long-term reduction in stress and allowing the horse to carry out a range of natural behaviours.

# 10 Riding

*'Whenever the horse stopped (which it did very often), he fell off in front; and whenever it went on again (which it generally did rather suddenly), he fell off behind.'*

Alice Through the Looking Glass, *Lewis Carroll*

What is the experience of being ridden like for the horse? A horse moves in the way he was born to move. Within hours of birth a foal can stand up, lie down, walk, trot and canter. The young horse in nature develops his muscles, speed, flexibility and co-ordination by moving to graze, stretching, playing and running from danger. At no point does a horse read a manual telling him where his head should be, how he should respond to the aids or how to perform a shoulder-in.

This chapter is not about how to ride. The aim is to look again at what we understand about the horse under saddle, and to consider the value of working outside the school in producing a ridden horse that can go on to work in any equestrian discipline.

# Movement – Natural or Unnatural?

Horses have always moved in the same way, yet human requirements of how we want them to move change constantly. Expectations have altered over centuries and across cultures, yet before 1877, when the horse's paces were photographed for the first time, we did not know how they moved. Seventeenth-century illustrations showing horses at liberty performing 'airs above the ground' and paintings of racehorses with all four legs extended are stylized artistic interpretations, not accurate depictions of natural movement.

Naturally, horses move in straight lines and wide curves. They do not tend to move in small, full circles. The pace they usually move at is a walk, mixed with occasional short bursts of trot, canter or gallop. Energy preservation is essential to survival, so trotting or cantering for long periods is not a rational activity. Horses meander along at a walk, stopping and starting, to look and graze. The horse naturally carries more of his weight on his front legs; the weight of a rider pushes the horse further on to the forehand. The process of the horse learning to carry a rider is, then, the process of the horse learning to balance himself with the change in weight distribution until he is eventually able to perform the movements we ask of him, in the way we desire.

High-school movements and jumping may be derived from natural movements, but they are not movements that most horses perform naturally and willingly. Think of the lengths that a horse will go to in order to avoid stepping over a pole on the ground. To a horse that depends on his legs for survival, what could be sillier than jumping a 1m (3ft) obstacle in the middle of a field, when he could just as easily go round? Those horses that do naturally perform the

■ **Modifying movement**
The sliding stop and turn of the bay horse in flight becomes formalized and repeated under saddle, putting great strain on the whole body. In natural situations, with wide-open spaces, horses would rarely need to pull up as suddenly as these horses are doing.

prances that we mould into dressage are usually highly aroused at that moment and do not spend more than a few seconds at a time doing so, and certainly not with the head in a vertical position and carrying weight on the back. Movements that involve elevation with little forward movement are not logical ways of expending energy, unless you are a posturing stallion. In this case, the motivation is reversed: the horse has a desire for movement but does not want to risk going forward too quickly in case a fight ensues.

Another factor to be borne in mind is that apparently simple requests from us may involve an unnat-ural action for a horse. We expect transitions from trot to canter when we ask for them but, naturally, horses make a transition in response to the force with which their feet are striking the ground. So, a horse moving naturally may trot faster and faster, then finally break into a canter, with no conscious thought involved. However, we expect the horse to canter when we say so and this is something we have to teach the horse, because to the horse the natural stimulus to canter is not there.

Due to physiology, physical training must be carried out over a long period of time. Physical development takes years. A horse in the wild is fully mature at about 11 years of age. Bones, muscles, ligaments and tendons take different lengths of time to strengthen – hence the problems experienced by racehorses, whose muscles are overdeveloped while tendons and bones are still weak. The implication of this for our training and riding is that we may need to rethink the age at which we start using a horse for various purposes, and also how we go about training.

**Training a horse to perform unnatural actions consists of two parts:**

1 The horse's body must be strong and supple enough to perform the required exercise.
2 The horse must learn to perform the required action at a cue from us.

# What is Collection?

■ **Lateral work**
This is trainer Charles Wilson with his dressage stallion. Although the horse performs a beautiful turn on the haunches with tack, practising with no reins or saddle helps the rider refine his aids.

■ **Flexion at the poll**
This 13-year-old ex-racehorse (right) has physical and emotional problems but is calmly learning the beginnings of collection in a rope halter.

In order to carry the weight of a human being without damaging himself, a horse needs to carry himself in a different way to when he is not mounted. The back needs to be raised, and this is achieved by bringing the hind legs farther forward underneath the body to support the extra weight. The muscles required to do this take time to develop and a horse that is forced into collecting will always physically resist because he is uncomfortable. A horse that is uncomfortable will have a tendency to raise his head and hollow his back, thereby suffering physical damage; a horse that is frightened will have the same reaction. In this situation, the psychological and physical state of the horse are inseparable.

Over the years, it appears that the understanding of collection has been lost in some quarters, with the focus being on what is occurring at the front of the horse – that is, the position of the head – rather than at the back end – that is, the hindquarters. Essentially, collection is the gathering of energy in the hindquarters in order to perform a particular action. Put very simply, this occurs when the muscles along the topline of the horse are extended and the muscles of the underside contracted. The position of the horse's head does not produce collection – it is the other way around.

For collection, several elements must be in place:

## 1 Free forward movement in a straight line

In order to gather energy, there has to be energy there. So, the first step in the long process of teaching a horse to collect is to get some energy into the hindquarters, and this is best done by encouraging active forward movement. Logically, to the horse, forward movement involves the head and neck being free. After all, the horse has usually been taught that backward pressure on the reins means stop.

Free forward movement is encouraged by riding out because the horse is interested in the process, particularly when taken over new country. His forward movement then comes from his own enthusiasm, so the rider does not have to resort to pushing a reluctant horse around a schooling area using legs, spurs and whips because the animal cannot see any reason to go forward. The aids can be taught while riding out — for example, asking the horse to stop and move off again at appropriate points.

Riders often worry that riding over rough terrain

**■ Spanish stallion ridden bareback in a headcollar**
In the photo above the rider is tense and leaning forward, holding on tightly to the horse's head. The stallion's stride is short, there is a lot of upward — rather than forward — movement, and his attention is not in the direction in which he is going. His head is restricted and held to one side. Imagine how much more uncomfortable the horse would be if he had a bit in his mouth.

In contrast, in the photo opposite the rider is relaxed and comfortable and the rein loose. The horse is going forward with enthusiasm, and his pricked ears show that his attention is to the front. Both horse and rider are much happier.

will damage their horses. In fact, built up over time it is an excellent way of developing the horse physically so that injury is *less* likely. It also teaches the horse to look where he is going and think about what he is doing. A horse will naturally go 'long and low' when given the freedom of the head and neck to do so. This stretching forward and down is the first stage in developing the muscles that are used when collection is required.

## 2 Circling and bending

Moving on circles and curves helps with collection because it encourages the horse to bring his hindlegs underneath him. However, this is difficult for a

young horse learning to balance under a rider. On a circle or curve, he has to bring his inside hind leg underneath him. Cantering on a circle is particularly challenging for an untrained horse.

When riding out, cantering can be introduced gradually. Once a horse can canter steadily on a straight line, large circles can be requested. As the horse adapts, both physically and mentally, to the task, smaller circles become possible.

Riding out also gives opportunities to teach lateral work. Opening and closing a gate is simply a series of turns on the quarters and on the forehand that encourage the horse to engage his quarters naturally as he learns the process (see page 103).

## 3 Engagement

If collection is seen as being necessary in order to perform a certain action — for example, to clear a jump — it is illogical to ask a horse, particularly an untrained one, to be collected when there is no action to perform. Contrary to beliefs in some quarters, a horse does not need to be in an 'outline' at all times. Having his head on the vertical will actually hinder him in most situations, especially out hacking over difficult terrain. If he is using his hindlegs to support the weight of the rider, and is relaxed and going forward, he is collected for the task at hand.

Working in a featureless schooling area gives the horse no clues as to the reason for performing actions. This can be overcome by introducing obstacles to work over and around. Riding out is also an invaluable part of the schooling process — after all, many showjumpers and eventers learn the basics when being hunted as young horses. Riding out helps with schooling because there are times when energy has to be concentrated into the hindquarters — to leap up a slope, for example. In this situation a horse has a *reason* to engage the hindquarters, and many cues can be taught in this way, by associating them with the horse's natural actions. With this type of riding the horse has to have freedom of the head and neck, and this in turn helps the rider to stop concentrating on the position of the head and focus instead on how the horse is using his whole body in order to complete the task required as comfortably and efficiently as possible.

# Position of the Horse's Head

Anna Sewell put the horse's perspective perfectly in *Black Beauty* when she wrote: 'Of course I wanted to put my head forward and take the carriage up with a will ... but no, I had now to pull with my head up, and that took all the spirit out of me and brought the strain on my back and legs.'

Fashions in the desired position for the horse's head change across time and cultures. Carriage horses used to have their heads strapped up; American walking horses have their necks up and heads pulled in. At present the trend is for the head to be vertical to the ground. The 'outline' is what we are told to aim for. The problem with concentrating on the outline or shape a horse makes is that we overlook what the horse is actually doing with his body. If we watch horses moving and playing at liberty, they rarely hold their head in one position. Are we saying that a horse in nature is never going correctly? The tendency to use the legs to drive the horse up into fixed hands may force the horse into an outline, but there will never be free movement and true collection. It also exacerbates any existing physical problems and may well cause new ones.

The optimum position for a horse's head will depend on many things, including the horse's conformation, his stage of physical development, natural tendencies such as flexibility, and the movement being performed. For example, Arabs naturally have a high head carriage (developed, it is said, to allow them to scan the desert horizons). Native cobs often have a low head carriage, an advantage in breeds that traditionally spent time trudging up mountains. Quarter horses carry their heads very low, a trait that has been bred into them because of its value when the horse is working cattle on a loose rein: the horse's eyes are at 'cow' level, his centre of gravity is low and he can swing his head to threaten the cow.

Discussions on whether the horse should be 'on the bit' or 'behind the bit' are widespread today, but there are many people riding horses without bits – and even without bridles – who achieve collection, so these terms are not used here. The central factor in the position of the horse's head is that relaxation and flexion at the poll are required. Currently, at all levels of riding, it is common to see the horse 'broken' somewhere along his neck, so that the 'break point' is higher than the poll and the front of the horse's face vertical to the ground or behind the vertical. This occurs because the horse is not truly collected and is unable to flex at the poll, due to tension and lack of training. Instead, the head has been forced down into what is considered the correct position using the reins or training aids. Because the horse has no option, he brings his head into position by putting a bend in his neck while retaining tension in the poll.

In reality, the position of the head depends on conformation and level of training. This means that the focus should be on whether the horse is working from behind, rather than on the position of his head and the tension on the reins. It makes little sense that some riders competing in dressage tests have been marked down for having too light a contact, even though the judges acknowledged that the horse was perfectly collected.

We must also bear in mind that forcing the horse to hold his head in a certain way may have negative effects and cause suffering. A horse needs freedom of his head in order to breathe properly. The action of the head moving up, back, forward and down assists in the expansion and contraction of the lungs. To get

## ■ Bearing rein

Still used in harness racing to encourage the horse not to break stride – it forces the horse's head up and back. Horses that raise their head and hollow the back when carrying a rider are similarly impeded, and muscle wastage along the back may result.

## ■ Draw reins

With his head levered down, the horse can do nothing to alleviate any discomfort. Equine physical therapists will testify to the damage done by draw reins, and eminent trainers warn that they should only be used in the most expert hands, if at all. The horse is totally at the mercy of the rider's hands. Should the horse stumble and the rider react by pulling on the horse's head, the horse may be levered on to his knees – just one reason why riding out in draw reins is actually dangerous.

## ■ Training aids

This is one of many pieces of tackle designed to force the horse into the position perceived as making it 'use itself'. Self-carriage cannot be forced but has to be developed over time. If used when riding and with an ill-fitting saddle, these devices can damage the horse's back and put strain on the cartilage of the sternum.

air in and out the horse needs the windpipe to be opened fully. This does not happen if the horse's neck is unnaturally bent. The soft tissues of the throat may produce obstruction when the horse is carrying his head vertically, sometimes resulting in gasping and roaring noises.

The horse also needs to be able to move his head in order to step out freely with the shoulder, because the large muscles of the neck are involved in pulling the forelegs forward.

### ■ Tight reins

This picture clearly shows the strain in the horse's neck muscles and the position of the windpipe. The mare's expression is typical of a horse with her head held in this position. Her attention, as revealed by the ears and eyes, is directed backwards, but she is not relaxed and listening to the rider – she is agitated and chewing on the bit. Many horses will pull against this use of the reins, resulting in the use of more martingales and other contraptions.

> **A horse needs his head free to be able to:**
> ■ Look and see.
> ■ Balance.
> ■ Breathe properly.
> ■ Use his back and neck properly.
> ■ Step freely.

## Effects of Bits and Nosebands

The horse needs his mouth unimpeded in order to swallow. Both horses and humans use their tongues for this. A horse whose mouth is full of foam from saliva produced while chewing the bit – something that we are told to encourage – cannot swallow if his tongue is compressed by the bit and his mouth is tied shut by the noseband. Similarly, a horse with a bit (or bits) that is too big for his

mouth will suffer in much the same way.

A horse that has his mouth tied shut and his head forced down is being suffocated. The result is panic, which is an understandable reaction in the situation. Once a horse begins to panic he will resist the rider and try to run away. Horses that heat up, becoming more agitated the longer they are ridden, may make some riders feel like good horsemen or women. The horse may be described as 'spirited' or 'a man's horse', but the reality is that he is actually fighting for the very air he breathes and, from his point of view, his life.

If a bit is carefully chosen to be comfortable for the horse and the rider truly uses it for communication rather than mechanical control, leaving the horse's

**■ The *serratón***
This device used in Spain consists of a double row of metal teeth, much like a bread knife, set inside a noseband. The horse is trained with reins attached to both the noseband and the bit. This horse has comparatively little damage; the difference between this and bit damage is that we can actually see this, and the resulting scar tissues. These devices are becoming available in other countries for controlling 'difficult' horses.

---

**A horse needs his mouth unimpeded in order to be able to:**
- Swallow.
- Avoid discomfort.
- Chew and relax the jaw.
- Touch and explore using his lips.

---

mouth alone as much as possible, the impediment to the horse is minimized.

## Communication or Control?

The bit is a piece of technology that has been with us for over 4,000 years. Is this because it is so perfect that it needs no development? Or is it because we actually know very little about how it works and what goes on in a horse's mouth? It is unfortunate for the horse that his mouth happens to be a shape that makes it possible for humans to tie a piece of metal into it. This would not work with a buffalo's mouth, or a camel's (although the normal instrument for guiding these animals, the nosepeg, is not particularly pleasant either).

The bit is intended to be a means of communica-

tion with the horse. However, although the bit is supposed to act on the bars of the mouth, horses frequently have a groove worn in their premolars, indicating that at times they hold the bit between their teeth. This may be because they like to play with the bit or to relieve discomfort, but the point is that when the bit is held between the teeth the communication from the rider's hand to the horse's mouth is being disrupted. In reality, the bit is not being used for communication but for mechanical physical control.

In the past, loriners would make bits to fit individual horses. There is now a return to the idea that

■ **Effect of a jointed bit**
This horse can do nothing to relieve the discomfort of the bit except open his mouth. Would tying his mouth shut actually solve the problem?

consideration must be given to the shape of the individual horse's mouth, rather than expecting that every horse should start in a snaffle and then move on to a stronger bit or more tack if the snaffle does not work. The idea that the bit is only to be used by a rider whose seat is balanced and independent of the hands is also becoming more popular, although forward-thinking trainers have always recommended that people learn to ride without a bit to begin with.

If we are going to use bits, we must be far more sensitive to the horse's reaction to them. The comfort of the horse needs to be addressed at all times. Certain ideas about humane bitting have been around for many years, but are ignored – for example, the recommendation that a snaffle bit should not be used with a martingale and drop noseband (see box).

**Snaffles, martingales and nosebands**
The nutcracker action of a jointed snaffle bit crushes the bars (gums) of the horse's mouth, making some horses open their mouths and raise their heads to avoid the discomfort. Once the head is raised, the action of the reins is downwards and the joint of the snaffle then pushes up into the roof of the mouth. Tying the horse's mouth shut removes his ability to reduce the pain by opening his mouth. A running martingale causes the rein to have a downward action sooner, and because the horse cannot raise his head, the discomfort is increased.

Alternatives to the bit include the hackamore, the bosal and the headcollar, and variations on these are available to give more choice and cater to individual differences. Once again, the organizations that govern competition need to change their fixed rules in order to enable people to use these alternative methods to communicate with their horses.

# The Rider's Posture

Being stable and balanced is the key to making riding comfortable for both horse and rider. We have all been shouted at about our position and told to put our legs further forward or further back. But the same applies to the rider as it does to the horse: we must understand what we are being asked to do, and be physically able to do it. Until we have ridden a horse that executes a perfect turn on the forehand, for example, how are we going to know what it feels like? Some people are naturally designed to wrap their legs around a huge warmblood while others are not.

■ **Ridden harmony**
A small boy on a large horse: the two of them are completely relaxed and enjoying a splash in the river.

There are several points we need to take into account:

## 1 Saddle design
One of the biggest barriers to achieving a balanced seat is the design of saddles. The saddle will put us into a certain position, irrespective of what we do to counter this. So before getting cross with ourselves, we need to consider if the saddle is actually a good design.

## 2 Horse's movement
A short-backed cob with an extravagant action may bounce up and down, with the knock-on effect of making the rider's lower leg swing. If we try to force our bodies into a certain position despite this

## Exercises: Being a Horse

### Walk downhill on a tight rein

1 Stand at the top of a short flight of steps (three or four is adequate, and make sure they are not too steep) then get down on your hands and knees.
2 Tuck your head down on to your chest.
3 Try walking down the stairs on hands and knees.

**Ask yourself**
☐ Can you see properly?
☐ Can you move properly?

4 Now repeat the exercise, this time moving your head and neck freely.

**Ask yourself**
☐ Is it any easier than the first time?
It is even more difficult for horses to move downhill on a tight rein. Their eyes are not positioned on the front of their head, so they see even less than we do in that position. In addition, while ridden they are carrying a weight that constantly moves, have to walk more than a few steps and cannot use their hands to grip.

### Walk uphill on a tight rein

1 Stand at the bottom of a steep slope.
2 Hold your hands behind your back, to simulate the effect of a tight rein on the horse's ability to use his shoulders and forelegs to pull him up the hill.
3 Try to walk or run up the slope.

**Ask yourself**
☐ What do you notice about your body position?

4 Now repeat the exercise with your arms free

**Ask yourself**
☐ How does your body position compare with the first time?
☐ Which is more difficult?
A horse needs his head, neck and shoulders free in order to move up a hill. When a horse's movement is being restricted by the reins he cannot move properly and, if willing to go, will compensate by misusing his body.

movement, we will set up tension. A long-backed Thoroughbred with a low, smooth action may make the same rider sit very differently.

### 3 Rider shape and posture

Everyone has a different body shape, different degree of mobility and different posture. We carry ourselves habitually, sometimes with tension and unevenness that will still be there when we get on a horse. We may sit with more weight to one side or the other, slump at the waist or be rigid. Our posture will have an effect on the horse, so it is our responsibility to achieve a balanced, relaxed seat that allows the horse to move because he is comfortable. We also need to remember that, due to individual differences in shape, size and posture, a good seat will not look exactly the same for every rider.

### 4 Emotions

Fear makes us tense and this is communicated to the horse. When we feel defensive, we go into the foetal position and lean forward. This is one of the surest ways to exacerbate problems when mounted. To become less afraid, we need to consider the suitability of the horse and/or our instructor.

Horses pick up on how we are feeling, so the mood in which we approach them will have consequences for their behaviour. If you are feeling stressed and impatient, it may not be the time to practise dressage. A ride out might both relieve your stress and avoid you giving the horse a bad experience by having a disagreement about schooling.

The answer to the question posed at the beginning of this section is that in order to ride well *from the horse's point of view* we need to be relaxed, know what our aim is, understand our horse and be able to communicate with him. These are the foundations from which enjoyable riding for both horse and rider can be built.

# Conclusion

*'Horsemanship: the act and art of riding, and of training and managing horses.'*

Collins Graphic English Dictionary, First Edition

In recent times, horsemanship has been packaged and sold in ways never seen before. Each horsemanship organization has courses, examinations, programmes and levels that can be followed. The market grows constantly, as more people fulfil their lifelong dream of owning a horse, then run into difficulties. Many of these difficulties arise from a lack of understanding of what kind of animal horses are and how they learn, and the belief that they can be bullied into doing what we want. Problems are created and compounded by intensive, unnatural horse-keeping practices.

There is nothing new in horsemanship, just new ways of presenting it – but simplistic, mechanistic approaches will never make us true horsemen or women. We have to truly understand the horse's psychology and physiology, and be able to interact with each horse as an individual. We have to make sure we do not replace brutal old methods with brutal 'new' ones. We need to put together an array of techniques that allows us to try different approaches in different situations.

The touchstone in horse training is that the horse is relaxed, attentive and understands what is being asked of him. The vision that most of us have of a perfect relationship with our horse will only become reality when the horse trusts us and chooses to follow our lead. To achieve this, we may have to put our own plans to one side: riding in that dressage test at the weekend or passing the next level of that course may not be possible. However, the rewards to be gained from developing true trust and co-operation are great, and the journey to reach that relationship fascinating in itself.

# Acknowledgements

I would like to thank the following people:

Lucy Rees, who has influenced my thinking for 20 years. James Hogg, Sue Hogg and Natalie Hogg, for reading and input – despite varying degrees of interest in horses. Rachel Bedingfield, for hours of discussion and many helpful suggestions. Francis Burton and Charles Wilson, for their expert reading and comment. Norman, Mandy, Chris and James Berry, and Lynne and Des Richardson, for allowing me to use their horses in case studies. Hannah Dawson, Paula Cox, Alison Rowan, Mark Rashid and Attila CseppentQ, for allowing me to use pictures of them and their horses. Sarah Widdicombe, for her fantastic input on editing, and the team at David and Charles.

Finally, all the horses, who make me constantly question what I think I know.

# Useful Addresses and Further Reading

## Useful Addresses

**British Equine Veterinary Association**
Wakefield House, 46 High Street, Sawston, Cambridgeshire CB2 4BG
tel: 01223 836 970    fax: 01223 835 287
www.beva.org.uk
*Provides a list of qualified equine dental technicians.*

**British Association of Equine Dental Technicians (BAEDT)**
www.equinedentistry.org.uk

**Equine Behaviour Forum**
Gillian Cooper, Carmel Cottage, Over Darwen, Lancs BB3 3JB
www.gla.ac.uk/External/EBF
*International non-profit organization to advance the sympathetic management of equines by promoting a better understanding of the horse's mind.*

**Equine Behavioural Rescue**
Abigail Hogg, c/o The Barn, Mankinholes, Todmorden, Lancs OL14 6HR
tel: 01706 839 059
www.equinebehaviouralrescue.co.uk
*Rehabilitates and rehomes 'problem' horses.*

**Horse-Centred Training**
Abigail Hogg, c/o The Barn, Mankinholes, Todmorden, Lancs OL14 6HR
tel: 01706 839 059
*Courses and consultancy in horse behaviour, horse keeping and training.*

**Natural Horse Group**
Stonefold Farm, Ilton, North Yorks HG4 4LA
tel: 01765 685 850
www.naturalhorsegroup.co.uk
*Membership organization to inform and educate on ways of improving the welfare of horses based on their natural needs.*

**Simple Systems Ltd**
Greenbank, Cherry Street, Duton Hill, Dunmow, Essex CM6 2EE
tel: 01371 870753/01728 604008
www.simplesystem.co.uk
*Supplies feeds that are free from cereals, molasses and additives; also offers pasture treatments, grass seeds and consultancy.*

## Further Reading

Berger, Joel, *The Horses of the Great Basin* (University of Chicago Press, 1986)
Budiansky, Stephen, *The True Nature of Horses* (Phoenix, 1998)
Fraser, Andrew F., *The Behaviour of the Horse* (CABI Publishing, 1992)
Holbrook Pierson, Melissa, *Dark Horses and Black Beauties* (Granta, 2000)
Kiley-Worthington, Marthe, *The Behaviour of Horses* (J.A. Allen, 1987)
——*Equine Welfare* (J.A. Allen, 1997)
Kurling, Alexandra, *Clicker Training for Your Horse* (Ringpress Books, 2001)
McBane, Susan, *How Your Horse Works* (David and Charles, 1999)
McCormick, A., & McCormick, M.D., *Horse Sense and the Human Heart* (Health Communications, 1997)
McGreevy, Paul, *Why Does My Horse?* (Souvenir Press, 2000)
Rashid, Mark, *Considering the Horse: Tales of Problems Solved and Lessons Learned* (Johnson Books, 1993)
——*Horses Never Lie: The Heart of Passive Leadership* (Johnson Books, 2000)
Rees, Lucy, *The Horse's Mind* (Stanley Paul, 1984)
Skipper, Lesley, *Inside Your Horse's Mind* (J.A. Allen, 1999)
Spark, Les, *Saddle Fitting for the Thinking Rider.* Available from Free 'n Easy Saddles, tel. 01943 850123.
Williams, Moyra, *Equine Psychology* (J.A. Allen, 1976)
Xenophon, *The Art of Horsemanship* (J.A. Allen, 1962)

## Picture Credits

David & Charles/Bob Atkins: pp2, 5, 33, 34, 37, 42, 56, 97, 104, 105, 123, 144 and front cover (back & lower lft)
Abigail Hogg: pp8, 19, 20, 23, 41, 54, 55, 59, 62, 67, 68, 69, 72–3, 82, 86, 87, 89, 92, 101, 106, 108, 109, 112, 114, 116, 124, 148, 149, 154,155;
Jim D. Hansen: p11;
Bob Langrish: pp12, 96, 145, 151 and front cover (top & lower rt);
Sarah Widdicombe pp14, 74, 90, 91, 94, 95, 115;
Jade Smith: pp28, 77, 125;
David & Charles/Matthew Roberts: p17
Linda Richardson: pp18, 46, 47;
Rachel Bedingfield: pp30, 45, 48, 49, 146, 147;
Sue Hogg: pp52, 76, 78, 152;
David & Charles/Bob Langrish: p58
David & Charles/Andrew Perkins: p80;
Amanda Berry: p83;
Fotograffs: p83;
James Hogg: pp121, 153
Kit Houghton: front cover (lower ctre)

Artworks by Maggie Raynor

# Index